Balance of Power,
Globalization and the Capitalist Peace

Ideas on Liberty

Balance of Power, Globalization and the Capitalist Peace

Erich Weede

liberal Verlag GmbH

Ideas on Liberty

**Balance of Power,
Globalization and the Capitalist Peace**

Erich Weede

Impressum:
1. Auflage, Januar 2005
© 2005 liberal Verlag GmbH, Berlin

Umschlag
Titelbild: Voller Ernst
Gestaltung: altmann-druck GmbH, Berlin

Satz und Druck: altmann-druck GmbH, Berlin
Printed in Germany – ISBN 3-920590-12-0

Contents

1. Preface 7
2. Balance of Power and War-Proneness 17
3. Globalization, Free Trade and
   the Division of Labor 27
4. The Capitalist Peace Between States 41
5. Capitalism, Democracy
   and the Avoidance of Domestic Conflict 61
6. Why We Need the Capitalist Peace,
   and Why We Can Afford It 81
7. What Must Be Done to Promote
   the Capitalist Peace 91
8. Conclusion 105
   Bibliography 111
   About the Author 141

Balance of Power, Globalization and the Capitalist Peace

1. Preface

The causes of war, and the prevention of war, have been my first research interests. My dissertation as well as my "Habilitationsschrift' (Weede 1975) focused on war and its avoidance. Since the late 1960s I never lost interest in war, although my interests expanded over time to include the development of capitalism and the rise and decline of nations or civilizations (Weede 1996, 2000) as well as the correlates and determinants of economic growth, income inequality, and rebellion or civil war. By the late 1990s these more recent interests threatened to push my older interest in war into the background.

But in late 2003 and early 2004 some conference obligations made me return to my older focus on war, and to connect it with my recent interests in capitalism and economic development. For a conference of the Standing Group on International Relations of the European Consortium on Political Research in Marburg in fall 2003 I wrote a review article of recent research on political violence (Weede 2004a). For a conference of the Mont Pelerin Society in Sri Lanka in January 2004 I wrote a paper on globalization and the capitalist peace (Weede 2004b). Although these papers – and, indeed, some earlier ones and chapters on globalization in recent books (Weede 1996, 2000, 2003) – already developed and defended the idea of a capitalist peace and welcomed the opportunity to spread it by globalization, they suffered from **not** embedding it in a wider theoretical perspective on the causes of war. An invitation to present yet another paper under the title of this small book to the European Regional Meeting of the Mont Pelerin Society in Hamburg in April 2004 provided the opportunity to remedy this shortcoming.

In contrast to earlier related papers I did not even try to publish the conference paper as a paper. By now, I had compiled enough ideas, theoretical propositions, and pieces of empirical evidence that a more comprehensive treatment made more sense than another short analysis of one or another aspect of the relationships between power balances and war, globalization or free trade and the prospect of making war less and less likely. That is why I gratefully accepted the invitation by Detmar Doering and the Liberal Institute of the Friedrich-Naumann-Foundation to publish a fairly comprehensive treatment of the topic which nevertheless should be accessible to general readers who do not make their living in practicing econometrics, quantitative research methods, or 'the scientific approach to world politics'.

If one does research or summarize the research of others – of course, most of the ideas, theories, and evidence discussed below have been produced by others – one cannot avoid some epistemological commitments. In the social sciences the fundamental choice is whether to pursue an ideographic or a nomothetic approach. Almost all historians choose the ideographic approach and focus on the description of structures or events, whereas most economists and psychologists choose the nomothetic approach and focus on the search for law-like general statements. Sociologists and political scientists are still divided – sometimes even by the Atlantic Ocean. In American political science the nomothetic approach dominates the flagship journal of the profession, the American Political Science Review, as well as more specialized journals, such as International Studies Quarterly, the Journal of Conflict Resolution, or World Politics. In German political science, however, the nomothetic approach has advanced little beyond electoral studies.

My own approach is definitely nomothetic. This is related to my training in psychology at one of the first German universities focusing on quantitative research methods in the early 1960s, the University of Hamburg. This epistemological orientation has been reinforced by graduate training in international politics at one of the first American universities emphasizing quantitative research in the late 1960s, Northwestern University, which is located in a suburb of Chicago.

Nomothetic research focuses on hypothesizing, testing and establishing law-like general statements or nomological propositions. Examples of such propositions are: The higher average incomes in a nation are, the more likely is democratic government. Or, the more economic freedom in a nation prevails, the less frequently it is involved in war. One characteristic of such propositions is that they say something about observable reality. Whenever you say something about reality, you risk that others find out that you are wrong. If we observed that most poor countries were democracies, but most rich countries were autocracies, then we should reject or, at least, modify the proposition about prosperity and democracy mentioned above.[1] Nomothetic researchers look for refutations. They try to falsify their propositions or theories (Popper 1934/1959). If the empirical evidence is compatible with one's theory, then one keeps the hypothetical propositions and regards them as supported – until negative evidence turns up. Although certitude about possession of the truth is beyond the capabilities of human inquiry, growth of knowledge is conceivable by the successive elimination of errors.

This epistemological approach borrowed from Popper would be easily applicable, if most of our propositions were deterministic, if they claimed to be valid without exceptions. Then, finding a single exception to a general statement – say, about prosperity and democracy – would suffice to falsify the proposition. Looking at poor India nevertheless being democratic, or at fairly rich Kuwait nevertheless being autocrat-

---

[1] A modification of a proposition frequently consists of specifying under which conditions it is valid, and under which conditions it does not hold.

ic, would suffice to reject the theory.[2] Unfortunately, almost no theory in macroeconomics, macrosociology, or international relations delivers deterministic propositions. Instead we have only probabilistic statements of the type that more prosperous countries are more **likely** to be democratic than others, or that economically freer countries are more **likely** to avoid war involvement than others. Probabilistic assertions never can be falsified by pointing to single events which do not fit with theoretical expectations. Instead we have to look at relative frequencies, at correlations or regression coefficients. We need statistical tools to evaluate such propositions. We typically ask the question whether a hypothesized relationship is so strong that it could only rarely occur because of random measurement or sampling error. Probabilistic propositions are regarded as supported only if they jump certain thresholds of significance which are ultimately defined by mere conventions.

Researchers are interested in causal propositions, that is, in statements about causes and effects, or determinants and consequences. Such statements can be used for explanation, forecasting, or policy interventions. We need to know more than the mere existence of some association or cor-

---

2   Here, it is not necessary to systematically distinguish between theory and propositions. It may suffice to say that a theory contains a number of propositions and some clarification of the logical relationships among propositions. In the social sciences outside of economics, the clarification of relationships between propositions tends to be fairly loose.

relation between, say, prosperity and democracy, or economic freedom and the avoidance of military conflict. We need to know whether prosperity **promotes** democracy, or whether democracy **promotes** growth, or whether, possibly, both statements might be defensible or, for the time being, taken for 'true'.

While a correlation between two variables, like prosperity and democracy, is equally compatible with the simple alternative causal propositions that prosperity causes democracy, and that democracy causes prosperity, this ambiguity no longer necessarily applies in more complex theoretical models. There, we tend to explain a single effect by a number of causes. For example, one may contend that democracy is promoted by prosperity as well as by a capitalist economic order (or economic freedom). We can take such a theoretical contention – which may be true or false, compatible with the data or not – as a starting point for specifying a regression equation.[3] If both theoretical statements – about the democratizing effects of prosperity and capitalism – were true, then the regression coefficients of both variables

---

3 All empirical tests have to rely on some assumptions. In practice, one never can test all the assumptions which one needs to make in order to test a falsifiable proposition. This is one out of many reasons why empirical tests can never result in certitude. Another one is that the techniques of data analysis themselves develop. Conceivably, better techniques might lead to different answers to our questions tomorrow. For a relevant recent debate about these issues, see de Marchi, Gelpi, and Grynaviski (2004) against Beck, King, and Zeng (2004).

should be positive and significant. If this is what we find in empirical research, then we regard the two propositions as provisionally supported. But final proofs remain impossible in empirical research. It is conceivable that some non-believer in the two propositions suggests a third measurable determinant of democracy. Before it actually is included in the regression equation, one never knows what its inclusion results in. Possibly, the previously significant and positive regression coefficients of prosperity and capitalism might be reduced to insignificance or even change signs. Then a previously supported causal proposition would have to be overturned and rejected.

The claim of causality implies more than observable association or correlation. It also implies temporal precedence of causes before effects. If one wants to test the causal proposition that prosperity contributes to democratic government, or that economic freedom contributes to the avoidance of military conflict, then one should measure prosperity or economic freedom before their hypothesized effects occur – certainly not later. If there is doubt about the direction of causality, as there frequently is, one might also look at the relationships between, say, earlier prosperity and later democracy as well as between earlier democracy and later prosperity. Although such investigations may become technically complicated, it might suffice here to keep the general principles in mind. From causal propositions we derive expectations about correlation or regression coefficients. But conclusions from correlations to causal propositions are not justified. One simply can never 'verify' causal statements by correlations. From causal propositions we also derive expectations about temporal precedence. As long as empirical evidence fits one's theoretical expectations, one regards the propositions or theory as provisionally supported and works with them.

There is another complication. As illustrated by the debate about the effects of trade and economic interdependence on the avoidance of military conflict below, full accordance of empirical studies and verdicts with theories is the exception rather than the rule – if it ever happens at all. That is why some philosophers of science (for example, Kuhn 1962; Lakatos 1968–69) have been critical of the idea of falsification and warned against premature rejection of propositions. If 'anomalies' or 'falsification' are more or less ubiquitous, then our task is no longer so easy as to choose between theories which have been falsified and therefore deserve rejection and those which are compatible with the facts and therefore deserve to be accepted **until** negative evidence turns up. Then our task becomes to choose between competing theories, for example about the conflict reinforcing or pacifying impact of trade, and to pick those which fit the data **relatively** better than others. So, the claim advanced in this review of the literature cannot be that the empirical evidence fits the capitalist peace idea perfectly, but merely that the evidence fits it **much** better than competing explanations of military conflict and notions about the negative impact of capitalism on the avoidance of conflict and war or the irrelevance of democracy do.

The epistemological discussion above could provide no more than a crude 'feel' for empirical research in the social sciences and its pitfalls. Although certitude is beyond reach, it is better to rely on testable, tested and so far supported propositions than on a hodgepodge of ambiguous hunches, contradictory thinking, and unsystematically evaluated empirical evidence.

Turning from method to substance, in this book I shall address the following issues: In the second section there is a sketch of a theory of power balances and war focusing on anarchy, security dilemmas, and territorial conflicts. Although capitalism, free trade and globalization seem to have no prominent place in this preliminary sketch, the third section of the paper deals with these topics in order to point out how free trade and globalization affect power balances and regime characteristics. The fourth section analyzes the capitalist peace, i. e., how free trade and democracy reduce war-proneness. In the fifth section, the issues of rebellion, political violence and civil war are analyzed. The capitalist peace seems to apply to intrastate conflicts as well as to interstate conflicts. In the sixth and seventh sections, it is discussed why we need the capitalist peace and what can be done to establish it. The final section provides a summary of the main propositions of this book.

2. The Balance of Power and War-Proneness

Wherever states or nations are capable of waging war against each other, wherever no effective superior authority is capable of imposing either the status quo or specific changes on all states within the international system including the most powerful ones, decision-makers face the prospect of war. That is why one of the leading thinkers on international security issues, Waltz (1979, p. 113), maintains: "In international politics force serves, not only as the **ultima ratio,** but indeed as the first and constant one." Those who do **not** prepare for waging war may have to face abdication and capitulation. Since this is not attractive to ruling elites, it is generally rejected. Given technical capabilities for waging war among states and the absence of an effective superior authority, there exists a 'security dilemma' (Herz 1950) for strategically interdependent states. Decision-makers in any rival pair of states believe to know that there is only one way to achieve security, i. e., superiority, preferably overwhelming superiority. This conceivable way out of the security dilemma may alternatively be labeled 'security by superiority' or 'peace by strength'. Of course, 'security by superiority' cannot work simultaneously for all contenders. Unless military technology provides defenders with a significant and persistent military advantage, even under surprise attack, superiority by one must necessarily imply inferiority and insecurity for others.

National security decisions are frequently made by groups instead of individuals. This imposes the necessity of within-group agreement or consent. 'Obvious' and 'familiar' solutions are likely to be chosen under collective decision-making, even if it is dubious that they work. 'Security by superiority' or 'peace by strength' is such an obvious or familiar solution to the security dilemma. If a better solution should exist, it will not necessarily be simple, sound familiar and therefore look reasonable. The immediate policy conclusion from 'peace by strength' is 'si vis pacem, para bellum' or 'if you want peace, prepare for war'. This conclusion has **not** lost its obviousness or attractiveness since Roman antiquity, although preparation for war frequently **did not** prevent its outbreak.

'Security by superiority' is not an equally obvious solution everywhere. The more military power a nation already commands, the more obvious 'peace by strength' and the 'prepare for war'-corollary appear. The more powerful one is, the more one attracts the resentment, suspicion and hostility of others. Under international anarchy, even wars of aggression may be perceived by their initiators as ultimately defensive for being preventive or preemptive. In this perspective, great power politics is a 'tragedy', "because there are no status quo powers" (Mearsheimer 2001, p. 2), except for hegemons who want to continue their dominance. The factual basis of this kind of 'offensive realism'[4] is the fact that initiators tend to win battles, campaigns, and in **some historical periods** even some types of war more frequently than their victims do (Betts 1985; Bueno de Mesquita 1981a; Dupuy 1987; Epstein 1988; for serious qualifications, see Wang and Ray 1994).

It is not only international anarchy or the security dilemma that carry the burden of explaining why states attempt to gain 'security by superiority'. Domestic politics matters, too. Expansionist policies are likely to affect individuals and interest groups within societies in different ways. Some may benefit, or seem to benefit. Others may expect nothing better than conscription, higher taxes, and the risk of being maimed or killed in war. Although it seems obvious that a majority of citizens and interest groups in most nations most of the time have little material interest in expansion and should be worried about expansionist policies, it is misleading to conclude from this that nations, or democratic nations, are never bellicose and expansionist. Snyder (1991, pp.15, 18) provides an explanation how even self-defeating policies may be agreed upon:

---

4   The dominant school of thought in international politics is called realism, sometimes with a big R. See Waltz (1979) for an authoritative statement of the defensive version of it. Mearsheimer (2001) has provided a reinterpretation of realism which he calls 'offensive realism'.

"Though overexpansion hurts the society as a whole, it is attractive to some groups within society. The benefits of expansion are disproportionately concentrated in their hands, while the costs of expansion are largely ... diffused throughout the society... Since interests in expansion and militarism are typically more concentrated than the interests opposed to them, logrolling is inherently more apt to produce overexpansion than underexpansion." This explanation must sound familiar to economists. In principle, public choice theory explains the voluntary subservience of elected politicians to special interest groups – including minority interests such as agriculture in contemporary Western societies – in the same way.

Constraints on national security decision-making also result from the polarity of the international system. What is perceived as possible and necessary depends on the system-wide distribution of power. One distinguishes between unipolar, bipolar and multipolar systems. By definition, a unipolar system is dominated by a single and hegemonic power. All other political units are severely constrained in their decision-latitude. Their sovereignty may approach the purely nominal. Economic growth and war serve to make, to maintain, or to break the preponderance of a hegemon. Given the immense superiority of the hegemon, the risk and difficulty of building a countercoalition that stands a chance of prevailing, and the obvious imbalance of power, unipolar systems are characterized by less frequent and shorter wars than other systems (Gilpin 1981; Modelski and Thompson 1993, p. 37; Organski 1958; Kugler and Organski 1993). In essence, anarchy and the security dilemma are mitigated or even overcome by unipolarity or hegemony. Whether bipolar or multipolar systems are more war-prone, however, is very much disputed (Bueno de Mesquita 1981b; Deutsch and Singer 1964; Kaplan 1957; Moul 1992; Singer, Bremer and Stuckey 1972; Waltz 1979).

National capabilities are the most important constraint on decision-making in security affairs. In the long run, such capabilities depend on growth rates. It has been persuasively argued that parity of power is associated with risks of war (Gilpin 1981; Organski and Kugler 1980). Quantitative research supports that preponderance pacifies, whereas parity is dangerous (Geller and Singer 1998, chapter 4; Kim 1992; Kugler and Lemke 1996; Lemke 2002; Moul 2003; Russett and Oneal 2001).[5] According to power transition theory, the risk of war is maximized under conditions of rough parity between hegemon and dissatisfied challenger or, more generally, between contending nations. Where some powers rise and others decline nobody knows the pecking order. Both sides may simultaneously entertain the illusion of superiority and believe that they might prevail in a military contest. Although power parity does not provide the motivation for war, it provides the opportunity for it. An

---

5 For a recent dissenting view, see Sweeney (2003).

essential part of the motivation must be the rejection of the status quo by some nation.

Most frequently the motivation is provided by territorial conflicts and aspirations (Goertz and Diehl 1992; Vasquez 1993; Weede 1975, 1996) or by the security dilemma and its policy implications. If all states accepted the status quo, then the rise and decline of nations or power transitions would not matter. Since the territorial status quo frequently has been determined by victory or defeat in previous wars, territorial grievances and challenges are always likely to exist. A similar ubiquity applies to the security dilemma. Therefore, the rise of challengers and the decline of defenders of the status quo is what makes conditions of parity or power transitions so dangerous to peace.

Power concentration is more likely to prevent war than power parity. Power concentration within pairs of nations interacts with power concentration at the international system level (Geller 1992). Where the system is characterized by a trend toward increasing concentration, or where the system moves from anarchy toward hegemony, the local pair-wise power balance matters much less than where the system is characterized by decreasing concentration. If there is a nation ascending toward or even maintaining hegemony, then local power balances among other nations hardly matter.[6] The hegemon is capable of constraining others. Where the system-wide power concentration is in the process of being reduced or where anarchy reasserts itself, there dyadic balances matter once again.

Although hegemony is one way to neutralize the severe and frequently irreconcilable conflicts of interest arising out of the security dilemma and the territorial delimitation dilemma, it is not the only one. Another one is the expectation of 'mutual assured destruction'. For most of the nuclear age most superpower leaders imagined nuclear war to be a great disaster where there would be no meaningful victor (Betts 1987). Under such conditions there may be 'peace through fear' (Aron 1966). Since the two superpowers of the Cold War period were allied with other nations, deterrence became extended to their allies or client-states as well. Take the example of both German states. According to the extended deterrence proposition, war between them has been prevented during the Cold War because both Germanies depended on one or the other superpower which did not want to risk 'mutual assured destruction' for the sake of their allies or clients. In this (testable) account (Weede 1975, 1983), the relationship between the two German states mattered least for the avoidance of war between them. What counted was dependence of both German states on 'their' superpowers, as well as nuclear deterrence between these superpowers.[7]

---

6 Consider the military balance between Central American 'banana republics' or Soviet client-states during the cold war. Political elites in these states know, or knew, that the military balance does not matter because no one can resist American arbitration in Central America, and no one could resist Soviet 'arbitration' in Eastern Europe.
7 Applying a very different approach, Adams (2003/2004, p. 77) provides further evidence for the pacifying impact of nuclear deterrence.

Another important determinant of national security results from geography. Since military power tends to decrease the further away from its home base a power is engaged (Boulding 1962), a central location in a configuration of powers is much more dangerous than a peripheral location (Bernholz 1985; Collins 1986). Obviously, insularity is the most peripheral and safest location which a nation may enjoy. By contrast, centrally located states have to worry about the capabilities of all their suspicious neighbors and to deploy forces against them. Any expansion of a central power soon becomes a threat to many other states, whereas a similar expansion of a peripheral state will cause worries much later and may even go unnoticed for some time. Therefore, geographically peripheral states stand a much better chance of transforming a multipolar system into a unipolar system with themselves as the hegemon or of becoming one of the dominant powers in a bipolar system than centrally located states.

It is no coincidence, but an illustration of the consequences of geopolitical configurations that the central power of the European state system, Germany, lost two world wars, that the insular powers, America and Britain, suffered least in these wars, and that two peripheral great powers, the Soviet Union and the United States, became contenders in the bipolar world after World War II. After the elimination of Germany as a great power in 1945 and after the rise of East Asia in the second part of the 20th century, however, the Soviet Union became the geopolitically central power of the interstate system. It suffered the usual and predictable consequences (Collins 1986, chapter 8; 1995) of encirclement by hostile states, in the Soviet case after 1969 even including the ideologically close People's Republic of China. Ultimately, the burden of competing against most of the rest of the world became too high. The Warsaw Pact and even the Soviet Union itself disintegrated.

3. Globalization, Free Trade and the Division of Labor

Since different economic growth rates obviously affect the balance of power, economics must not be neglected in an analysis of balance of power politics. Besides, the character of domestic regimes is not as irrelevant for the analysis of war-proneness as the incomplete sketch provided above seems to suggest.

The process of globalization had already begun in the late 19th century (Lindert and Williamson 2001). Before World War I, trade and foreign investment were fairly globalized. Because of low political obstacles to international migration, labor markets actually were more globalized at the beginning of the 20th century than at its end. The two World Wars, the Great Depression in between, and the temptations of socialism, planning, and autarchy interrupted the process of global market integration for about half a century. Thereafter, the process regained force and speed. Now, cheap, fast and reliable communication and transportation enables producers of goods and some service-providers in low-wage countries to challenge high-cost producers in rich countries on their home turf. But technological innovation resulting in falling prices and rising speed of intercontinental communication and transportation is **not** the only determinant of globalization.

Globalization also resulted from the insight that collectivism, planning and socialism, simply do **not** work. According to Lindsey (2002, p. 9): "Globalization is not a simplistic technological imperative... It is the retreat of the state that has allowed international market relationships to regain a foothold. This retreat was provoked, not by the impingement of blind economic forces or transports of libertarian enthusiasm, but by disillusionment. The (socialist, E.W.) dream died because it failed. It failed morally in the horrors of its totalitarian variants; and it failed economically by miring millions in grinding poverty and subjecting billions more to unnecessary hardships. Globalization is the fitful, haunted awakening from the dream." Political decisions in rich and poor countries alike contribute strongly to globalization. Tariffs and, to a lesser degree, non-tariff barriers to trade have been reduced. Entrepreneurs in many countries try to find and to exploit their comparative advantage, to realize economies of scale and gains from trade by looking for buyers and sellers everywhere. If trade between countries is truly free, then it promises to enrich all nations.

By definition, globalization refers to global economic interdependence. Although enlightened American policies after World War II – very much in contrast to American policies in the 1930s – did contribute to the liberalization of trade within the West, although some imperfect approximation to free trade made the recovery of West Germany and Japan possible as well as the later economic miracles in the East Asian tiger economies, any globalization deserving the label has to include the demographic giants on earth, that is, China and India where about 40 % of mankind live. In China's case, the opening was pushed by an enlightened communist, Deng Xiaoping. He was the first powerful leader of a socialist nation to understand that socialism simply does **not** work. Similarly, market oriented reforms in India already began under the leadership of the same Congress Party which was inspired by the Soviet economic model for about four decades. As in China, the 'conversion' to capitalism in India was incomplete and rooted in previous failure and the necessity of reform resulting there from (Lindsey 2002; Weede 2000, chapters 4 and 6).

The process of globalization still is far from complete (Lindsey 2002; Theurl 1999, p. 72). Many economies still suffer from a legacy of collectivism and planning. There remain significant price differences between countries even in internationally traded goods. Domestic savings and investments remain correlated. Even among international investors there is some home bias. Much international investment is not motivated by differences in labor cost, but by hopes of serving foreign markets. Foreign direct investment did not exceed 5 % of GDP in major economies during the last decade of the twentieth century. More than 80 % of production in most major economies still was destined for domestic consumption and more than 80 % of investment still was financed by domestic investors (Wade 1996, p. 61).

Free trade has costs and benefits attached to it. By overcoming borders and distance globalization must reinforce the most important characteristic of capitalist or market economies, i. e., competition resulting in 'creative destruction' (Schumpeter 1942). Even oligopolies do not necessarily reduce competition and innovation. It has been argued that oligopolistic competition in free markets maximizes innovation because no one can afford **not** to innovate (Baumol 2002). In capitalist economies competition may start to bite before it exists. Not only competition itself, but the mere threat of future competition may generate attempts at innovation and cost-cutting. Where competition and innovation are not stifled by politics, bankruptcies occur and some workers lose their jobs. In principle, no one is safe for ever. Many people resent being condemned to an ever-lasting effort to remain competitive. Moreover, resentment about the need to retain competitiveness might grow, the more one lives in material comfort and the more established the welfare state is.

Without the innovation generated and imposed by competition, mankind would still be poor. Most of the benefits of innovation are not even appropriated by innovators, but by consumers. Whether or not one agrees with Baumol (2002) on the egalitarian impact of competition and innovation, they certainly overcame mass poverty first in the West and then in the newly industrializing countries of Asia.

Globalization cannot be reduced to free trade. But free trade is certainly an essential part of it. Before looking at the material benefits of free trade one might also look at its intellectual benefits. Since trade necessitates human interaction, it also promotes some diffusion of ideas. Although this spread of ideas may be only an unintended consequence in many instances, one may nevertheless agree with Landes (1998, p. 136) who has argued: "If the gains from trade in commodities are substantial, they are small compared to the trade in ideas." After all, it is hard to imagine what one might learn from somebody who knows exactly the same things as one already knows oneself. But is easy to imagine learning from somebody who is different in interests, knowledge, skills and intellectual perspective. By promoting interaction across borders, globalization necessarily promotes opportunities for cognitive transfers, for intellectual exploration and the growth of knowledge. The importance of this diffusion of ideas may be illustrated by examples from the past: by the West 'importing' so-called Arab numbers ultimately from India, by the West re-importing even a major part of the Greek philosophical heritage from the Arabs, by the spread of Buddhism from India via China to Japan, by the 'export' of Western commercial law to Singapore and increasingly to Mainland China, and by the 'export' of democracy to the doorsteps of the Chinese Mainland, that is, to South Korea and Taiwan.

The cosmopolitan interest in free trade rests on two solid foundations. Free trade is in the welfare interest of mankind.[8] If one defines the (economic) national interest by something related to the greatest good for the greatest number, by high and growing average incomes, then there can be little doubt about free trade being part of the national interest, too. Benefits from free trade do **not** even depend on reciprocity (Bhagwati 1991, p. 51). The national interest requires invigorating one's entire economy, not getting away with protection for some special interests or specific industries. Nevertheless, multilateral trade negotiations may be useful in mobilizing the support of exporters and therefore in balancing the protectionist lobbying of those industries which have to compete with imports (Irwin 2002, p. 167).

In principle, globalization permits a global division of labor. Since the days of Adam Smith (1776/1976) we know that the size of the market limits the division of labor, that the division of labor boosts innovation and productivity. In principle, globalization is the logical endpoint of an economic evolution that began when families changed from subsistence farming and household production to production for the market. As long as globalization is not yet completed, there remain gains from trade to be realized by further market expansion. We are still far from a state of affairs where customers are as likely to buy from a foreign as from a domestic source. For US customers, such a state of affairs would mean an import

---

8 Sometimes it is argued that globalization threatens welfare states and generates a 'race to the bottom'. First, there is little empirical evidence to support this view (Rodrik 1998; Lindert 2004, pp. 186, 223). Second, this argument rests on the assumption that the welfare state is valuable in itself – in spite of its tendency to curtail individual freedom.

share of GDP about **six times** as high as the share at the end of the second millennium (Irwin 2002, p. 18).

Since globalization adds to competitive pressure, since it reinforces the 'creative destruction' inherent in capitalism (Schumpeter 1942), it causes resentment. Since globalization is fed by technological innovation and political decisions promoting free trade, these innovations and decisions attract resentment, too. The world is already globalized enough that national resistance to innovation by most nations does little harm from a global perspective. It 'merely' affects the rise and decline of nations. The US is the only nation whose power **might** suffice to derail the process of globalization.

Free trade is politically vulnerable. If foreigners are perceived as a cause for the need to adjust, then attacking free trade becomes politically attractive. After all, no politician benefits from the affection of foreigners who cannot vote in his constituency. Of course, those economists who insist on the benefits of free trade – **even** if your partner does **not** practice free trade – are right. Benefits include serving customers better at lower prices, but also total factor productivity growth (Edwards 1998). Free trade has little effect on the level of employment. But it does facilitate **productive** employment (Irwin 2002, chapter 3). Although even in manufacturing, churning, or the movement of workers from one job to another one, dominated downsizing in America, although the much larger service sector of the American economy actually added jobs during the recent period of globalization (Baumol, Blinder, and Wolff 2003), downsizing has been more visible than churning.

Benefits to consumers from globalization tend to be overlooked. The benefits of free trade tend to be dispersed widely, the costs of it – for example, in bankruptcies and job losses – tend to be concentrated and more visible. Therefore, the political case against free trade may become very strong despite the weakness of the economic argument. Since people react psychologically more strongly to losses than to gains – even by risk-acceptance in a gamble to avoid the loss altogether (Kahneman and Tversky 1979) – there is another incentive for politicians to turn protectionist. Although Western societies after World War II by and large succeeded in containing rampant protectionism – except for European and Japanese agriculture and the multifiber agreement regulating the textile and apparel trade – protectionism remains a permanent temptation.

There is a dispute about the degree to which either trade or technological progress is responsible for the predicament of unskilled labor in the West. While the majority view (e.g. Krugman 1996) blames most of it on technological progress, this is not entirely satisfying, because technological progress is frequently inferred from residuals rather than directly measured. An outspoken minority (e. g. Wood 1994, pp. 166–167) puts most of the blame on free trade and estimates that about 9 million manufacturing jobs had been lost in rich countries already by 1990 and many many more by now. The complimentary gain of 23 million jobs in poor countries may satisfy our humanitarian impulses, but it does not help Western politicians to win elections. In the last three years one out of six manufacturing jobs had been lost in the United States (Economist 2003a, p. 30). Americans look for scapegoats, although trade is almost certainly **not** the major determinant of these job losses. Improvements in productivity in themselves imply less employment in those sectors of the economy, like manufacturing, where productivity grows better than elsewhere. Since China has a larger trade surplus with the US than even Japan, China-bashing has become popular in America.

As prosperous countries make better trade partners than impoverished ones, as economic freedom promotes prosperity, trading states **should** recognize a 'selfish' interest in the freedom and prosperity of other nations. Hayek (1960, p. 32/1971, p. 41–42) has pointed out, the 'selfish' interest in the freedom and prosperity of others applies to individuals within societies as well as to nations or states: "The benefits I derive from freedom are thus largely the result of the uses of freedom by others, and mostly of those uses of freedom that I could never avail myself of. It is therefore not necessarily freedom that I can exercise myself that is most important to me… The benefits of freedom are therefore not confined to the free – or, at least, a man does not benefit mainly from those aspects of freedom which he himself takes advantage of. There can be no doubt that in history unfree majorities have benefited from the existence of free minorities and that today unfree societies benefit from what they obtain and learn from free societies. Of course the benefits we derive from the freedom of others become greater as the number of those who can exercise freedom increases."

Unfortunately, our interest in the freedom and prosperity of others does not guarantee that we behave accordingly. Our common long-term interests are frequently neutralized by short-term politics. As Drezner (2004, p. 31) has observed: "the benefits of free trade diffuse across the economy, but the costs of trade are concentrated. Thus, those made worse off by open borders will form the more motivated interest group" – and prevail.

Recently, the Bush administration supported a farm bill in 2002 which provides more subsidies for American agriculture and at the same time increases the US budget deficit. In the same year Chirac persuaded Schröder to postpone for another decade serious attempts to reduce agricultural subsidies in the European Union. Rich country agricultural policies deprive poor countries of export markets. Western countries do not even desist from harming agricultural producers, such as West African cotton producers, who survive on a dollar per day (Campbell 2004, p. 112). Similarly, the Bush administration imposed tariffs on imported steel from March 2002 to December 2003 in order to protect American steelworkers. Since steel-users employ a multiple of the number of workers employed in producing steel, it has been estimated that **at least** 45000 jobs were lost because artificially high steel prices undermined the competitiveness of some American steel-using industries (Drezner 2004, p. 33).

Like technological progress, free trade exacts the price of necessitating structural adjustment which may be onerous to some. Restricting free trade, however, would condemn some workers to unnecessarily low productivity and correspondingly low wages. Trade is not even the main culprit of the predicament of low-skilled labor in such countries.[9] If it were, the relative wages of educated workers in many developing countries should not have increased as they did (Irwin 2002, p. 99). It is much easier to explain rising relative wages of educated workers in poor and rich countries alike by technological change than by free trade or globalization. But the mere fact that **some** economists explain growing inequality or unemployment[10] in rich countries by free trade (as **one** among other causes) does increase the political vulnerability of free trade. Whoever loses a job or some part of a wage asks politicians for remedy, preferably immediately. As long as some degree of protection promises some immediate

---

9 According to Bhagwati (2004b, pp. 124–127), trade with poor countries may even have improved real wages in the US, and US protectionism might hurt American workers and the poor in their capacity as consumers.
10 According to Irwin (2002, p. 71), "the overall effect of trade on the number of jobs in an economy is best approximated as zero." Trade reallocates jobs without significantly affecting their number.

results, it looks attractive, quite independent of the soundness or even sanity of the economic reasoning behind protectionist moves.[11] Whereas American elites endorse globalization and free trade, the American public remains skeptical. According to Huntington (2004, p. 13), "four-fifths of the public but less than half of foreign policy leaders think protecting American jobs should be a 'very important goal' of the U.S. government." Not only in Continental Europe, but also in America there is a pool of anti-globalization views waiting to be exploited by nationalist and populist politicians. Unfortunately, protectionist policies frequently harm employment in other domestic industries by raising their production costs because much foreign trade is in intermediate components and parts.

The purpose of free trade is to make all countries better off. It is **not** to preserve any existing hierarchy of power or hegemony. If free trade coexists with advantages of backwardness, then there may be leveling world order effects. Stein (1990, p. 139) recognized this more than a decade ago: "A hegemonic power's decision to enrich itself is also a decision to enrich others more than itself. Over time, such policies will come at the expense of the hegemon's relative standing and will bring forth challengers. Yet choosing to sustain its relative standing ... is a choice to keep others

---

11 For a criticism of such remedies as 'countervailing duties' and 'anti-dumping' procedures, see Irwin (2002, chapter 4).

impoverished at the cost of increasing its own absolute wealth."

Unfortunately, at least one influential American strategist argues in favor of keeping some others impoverished. According to Mearsheimer (2001, p. 4), "China and the United States are destined to be adversaries as China's power grows." If one relies on this pessimistic assumption, then Mearsheimer's (2001, p. 402) conclusion is unavoidable, then "the United States has a profound interest in seeing Chinese economic growth slow considerably in the years ahead."[12] Since hundreds of millions of Chinese still have to survive on about a dollar per day, an American desire to reduce Chinese growth rates must be perceived as hostile. Keeping hundreds of millions of people close to the starvation level would not be a humanitarian policy. But it would also be incompatible with the Western objective to promote a pacific world order.

---

12 Mearsheimer's view might even imply the policy recommendation of an American preventive war against China, although Mearsheimer hesitates to be explicit about this implication of his theory. Fortunately, however, the preventive motive seems to generate few wars (Lemke 2003).

4. The Capitalist Peace Between States

In my view, the economic benefits of globalization and free trade – although real – are **much less** important than the international security benefits. The quantitative literature comes fairly close to general agreement on the following four propositions from political economy, political sociology and international relations: First, democracies rarely fight each other (Ray 1995; Russett 1993; Russett and Oneal 2001).[13] This does not necessarily say that democracies

---

13 Technically, this finding of democracies only rarely (if ever) fighting each other derives from cross-dyad variation, not from cross-time variation which might be insufficient to produce strong effects (Ray 2003, pp. 25–26). One of the most forceful criticisms of the democratic peace proposition has been advanced by Gowa (1999). In her view, one should not aggregate the data over extremely long periods of observation, as Russett (1993) and his colleagues (Russett and Oneal 2001) have done. If one analyzes different periods of history separately, then there is little support for the democratic peace before 1945. Since there have been relatively few stable and contiguous democracies before World War II, the acceptance of Gowa's empirical criticism is not very damaging to the democratic peace proposition. When the democratic peace applied to few contiguous (and therefore war-prone) dyads or pairs of nations, then one should not even have expected significant pacifying effects.

fight fewer wars than other regimes. It is even compatible with the until recently widely shared view that the risk of war between democracies and autocracies might be even higher than the risk of war between autocracies.

An early explanation of the relationship between democracy, as we say today, or republicanism, as he would have preferred to say, and peace, has been provided by Kant (1795/1963, pp. 94–95)[14]: "If the consent of the citizens is required in order to decide that war should be declared ... nothing is more natural than that they would be very cautious in commencing such a poor game, decreeing for themselves all the calamities of war. Among the latter would be: having to fight, having to pay the costs of war from their own resources, having to repair the devastation war leaves behind, and, to fill up the measure of evils, load themselves with a heavy national debt that would embitter peace itself and that can never be liquidated on account of constant wars

---

14 In German one finds this quote in Kant (1795/1964, pp. 205–206). Immediately thereafter there is a discussion of republics and democracy. By and large, Kant appreciates republics defined by a distinction between the legislative and executive branches of government, but he is critical of democracy because of its despotic temptations. If democracies are characterized by checks and balances and by limited government – as most contemporary democracies (still) are (in spite of excessive regulation and taxation) – then they simultaneously remain republics. Since this is not a treatise on Kant and his political philosophy, I believe it to be permissible to downplay his distinction between republics and democracies.

in the future." This type of theorizing would make one expect that democracies are less inclined to fight and therefore fight fewer wars than other nations do. One may add that neither institutions nor norms easily explain why only democracies benefit from democratic pacifism. In addition to the costs of war, or instead of the costs of war, either institutional constraints, that is checks and balances, or the acceptance of pacific norms might be the main determinant of democratic pacifism (Dixon 1993; Maoz and Russett 1993; Owen 1994; Zinnes 2004). Why democratic pacifism might only apply to relations between democracies has been suggested by Doyle (1993, p. 33): "Because nonliberal governments are in a state of aggression with their own people, their foreign relations become for liberal governments deeply suspect. In short, fellow liberals benefit from a presumption of amity; nonliberals suffer from a presumption of enmity. Both presumptions may be accurate. Each, however, may also be self-fulfilling."

Possibly, the most persuasive explanation of peace among democracies is Lipson's (2003) theory of reliable partnership. His theoretical starting point is the idea that war is a waste of resources and that every participant in war could become better off if the bloody waste could be avoided. In Lipson's (2003, p. 49) own words: "Hypothetically at least, an agreement could yield more to everyone because it would eliminate the costs and risks of war. Both winners and losers would receive whatever they could get in the gamble of war, plus some share of the resources that would otherwise be wasted in fighting. Everyone would be better off, a Pareto-superior solution. If such a solution is available, then why do we sometimes fail to grab it?" In Lipson's view, autocracies suffer from a contracting disadvantage. Bluffing is too easy for them. Unexpected strikes are too easy for them because of a political culture of secrecy. Neglecting their commitments is too easy for them. Democratic transparency and constitutional procedures, however, make contracts and commitments more difficult to arrive at, but also more credible and persistent. Lipson (2003, p. 47) regards the democratic contracting advantage as "the fortunate by-product of institutional arrangements designed to give citizens control over their leaders. They are the unintended consequence of structures devised for domestic purposes. Democratic policy processes, for example, are open to public view, subject to challenges from opposition parties, and scrutinized by a free press and other branches of government. In a world where news travels instantly, giving this information to voters, elected officials, and journalists also gives it to other states. That makes democracies inherently more transparent than dictatorships, traditional monarchies, or one-party states."

It is important to distinguish here between less well established and strongly supported claims about the democratic peace. There is little doubt that democracies almost never fought each other, least of all after World War II. There is still some debate, however, whether democracies are as frequently and as bloodily as other states or less frequently and less bloodily involved in military conflict and war than autocracies (Benoit 1996; Bremer 1992; Chan 1984; Rummel 1995; Weede 1984). Above all, I focus on the weaker claim that democracies tend to be pacific among themselves which received much more solid support than the general claim about democratic pacifism. The strongest doubts about democratic pacifism have recently been suggested by Waltz (2003–2004, p. 181) when he began with a simple observation and ended with a very disquieting interpretation of it: "The weaker can hardly threaten the stronger, yet democratic countries go to war against them. If this is true, it tells us something frightening about the behavior of democratic countries; namely, that they excel at fighting and winning unnecessary wars." So, one of the reasons for my skepticism about the pacifist inclinations of democracies concerns the frequencies of wars between major powers, democracies included, and autocratically ruled minor states. The recent wars between the United States and the United Kingdom against Saddam Hussein's Iraq may serve as illustrations. The second reason concerns the inclination of great powers, including democracies, to consider and occasionally to wage preventive or preemptive wars. Here, not only the most recent war against Iraq is an illustration, but also American considerations of preventive or preemptive war against China under Kennedy and Johnson because of China's progress in developing nuclear weapons during the 1960s (Goldstein 2003). Finally, most quantitative studies concerning democracy and peace did not include an analysis of colonial wars. Although this does not affect the dyadic democratic peace proposition – because colonial territories were not democratically ruled before or under colonialism – it raises some serious questions about the generally pacific character of democracies as such.

Second, prosperity or high per capita incomes promote democracy (Burkhart and Lewis-Beck 1994; Lipset 1994; Przeworski et a. 2000; Boix and Stokes 2003). Again, some details of the relationship are still disputed, but the relationship itself and the fit between a causal interpretation of it and the temporal ordering of the data are no longer debatable. Przeworski et al. (2000) argue that rising incomes do not make the transition from autocracy to democracy more likely, but rising incomes prevent the backward transition from democracy to autocracy. Obviously, transitions to democracy become more valuable if they are permanent rather than transient episodes. Higher per capita incomes do contribute to the permanence of those democratic transitions which happen. Recently, however, Boix and Stokes (2003) provided econometric evidence that economic growth does cause autocracies to democratize, too.

Third, export orientation in poor countries and open markets in rich countries, i. e., trade between rich and poor countries promotes growth and prosperity where it is needed most, in poor countries (Bhalla 2002; Collier and Dollar 2002; Dollar 1992; Dollar and Kraay 2002; Edwards 1998; Lindert and Williamson 2001, p. 37). Fourth, (bilateral) trade reduces the risk of war between (dyads of) nations (Oneal and Russett

1997, 1999; Oneal, Russett and Berbaum 2003; Russett and Oneal 2001). Actually, the pacifying impact of trade **might** be even stronger than the pacifying impact of democracy (Oneal and Russett 1999, p. 29; Gartzke 2000, p. 209).[15]

Of course, there are dissenting voices in the literature, too (Barbieri 2002; Beck, Katz and Tucker 1998).[16] Barbieri's results have become less worrisome and largely explainable because of recent findings. As Oneal and Russett (2003a, p. 160; 2003b, p. 184; and Oneal 2003, p. 723) recently demonstrated, the pacifying impact of trade is maximized where the analysis is focused on disputes with fatalities rather than on non-lethal conflicts, or where the focus is on contiguous dyads or dyads including a major power rather than on those dyads where the risk of military conflict is close to zero to begin with. Alternatively, great power status and distance have to be controlled in order to avoid erroneous conclusions (Gartzke and Li 2003c). As Gartzke and Li (2003a) demonstrated, dyadic trade shares relative to the

---

15 Changing the dependent variable from 'militarized disputes' to 'international crises', Hewitt (2003) disagrees. In his analyses trade looks less pacifying than democracy or international organizations and just fails to reach the significance threshold.

16 Beck, Katz and Tucker raised the serious issue of time dependence in the time-series-cross-section data. But Russett and Oneal (2001; Oneal and Russett 2003b) made successful efforts to respond to the methodological criticism raised against their earlier work.

size of national economies (rather than relative to national trade) do reduce the risk of military conflict. In operationalizing variables and specifying equations, Barbieri consistently chose the options minimizing the pacifying impact of trade. Moreover, even Barbieri (2003; Barbieri and Peters 2003) herself found some pacifying impact of economic freedom or openness to trade on the one hand and the war involvement of nations on the other hand.

Finally, Hegre (2000) found that 'peace by trade'-effects are stronger among developed than among less developed countries. Possibly, nations have to grow out of poverty before they can reap the peace dividend of trade. Later, however, he and his co-authors (Mousseau, Hegre and Oneal 2003) found that the pacifying effects of trade, but **not those of democracy** apply irrespective of the level of economic development. Hegre (2004, p. 427) also investigated whether size asymmetry and different national degrees of trade dependence affect the pacifying impact of trade and arrived at the following conclusions: "The analysis clearly supports the general finding that high levels of trade are associated with low probabilities of conflict... Breaking down barriers to trade has only a negligible impact on the probability of conflict in relations between states of very different size. On the other hand, the empirical analysis reported here indicates that conflicts are most likely in symmetric dyads... Trade is thus reducing conflict most for the most conflict-prone dyads." Mansfield and Pevehouse (2003) suggested another modification of the 'peace by trade'-

proposition. In their view, institutions such as preferential trade arrangements reinforce the pacifying impact of trade. According to Gartzke and Li (2003b, pp. 578–579; Gartzke 2004), capital market integration **might** be even more effective in reducing the risk of military conflict than integration of goods markets or trade.

As with the democratic peace, one might ask **why** economic interdependence or trade might reduce the risk of military conflict and war. Again, I feel that the answer to this **why** question cannot be given with the same amount of confidence as the question **whether** trade or interdependence promotes peace. One can either point to cost-benefit calculations or to the effects of interdependence on signalling. Cost-benefit arguments may point to the costs of disruption of trade. Or, they may point to the necessity to assure access to raw materials or markets by either commercial or military means. Blocking commercial access might make political leaderships look for aggressive alternatives (Hale 2004, p. 143). But there might also be positive political externalities of economic globalization. Gartzke and Li (2003b, p. 561) have argued: "Global integration of economic markets may also reduce uncertainty by making talk costly ex ante. Autonomous global capital can respond dramatically to political crises. To the degree that globalization forces leaders to choose between pursuing competitive political goals and maintaining economic stability, it reveals the intensity of leader's preferences, reducing the need for military contests as a method of identifying mutually acceptable bargains." For my purposes, neither the compatibility nor the comparative validity of such claims need be answered. These issues can be left to future research.

Trade or economic interdependence plays a pivotal role in the prevention of war, because it exerts direct **and** indirect pacifying effects. In addition to the direct effect, there is the indirect effect of free trade on smaller risks of military conflict mediated by growth, prosperity, and democracy. Since the exploitation of gains from trade is the essence or purpose of capitalism and free markets, I label the sum of the direct and indirect international security benefits "the capitalist peace", of which "the democratic peace" merely is a component.[17] Even if the direct 'peace by trade'-effect **were** eliminated by future research, economic freedom and globalization would still retain their crucial role in overcoming mass poverty and establishing the prerequisites of the democratic peace. That is why I (Weede 1996, chapter 8) already advocated a capitalist peace strategy before Oneal and Russett (1997, 1999) convinced me of the existence of a directly pacifying effect of trade.

---

17 Since I have heard the term 'capitalist peace' before, I cannot claim that it is my own invention. But it is a felicitous term. Russett and Oneal (2001) refer to a Kantian peace instead which is built upon three components : the democratic peace, peace by trade, and peace by collaboration in international organizations (or IGOs). The IGO element of the Kantian tripod looks weakest and least robust to me. Gartzke (2004, pp. 2, note 7, and 33) also doubts the pacifying impact of IGOs.

Moreover, capitalism and economic freedom affect democracy not only via their impact on prosperity. Another part of this relationship derives from the fact that only the capitalist divorce of economic and political power permits dissent. Without opportunities for dissent democracy cannot exist. Whether people will dare to dissent depends on the cost of doing it. According to Bhagwati (1993, p. 34): "The cost of dissent is immense when those who hold political authority also control the means of production." Although capitalism or economic freedom is **no sufficient** condition for democracy, it might be a **necessary** one.

The direct pacifying effects of trade seem to be about as strong as those of democracy. Because of their contribution to prosperity, capitalism and free trade also do underwrite democracy, and thereby the democratic peace where it prevails. Moreover, peace by trade does not suffer from a geopolitical complication which affects peace by democratization. According to some research, the risk of war between democracies is much lower than elsewhere, but the risk of war between a democracy and an autocracy is higher than elsewhere – at least in recent decades.[18] If one attributes causal significance to these observations, as I do, then democratization does **not** contribute to peace everywhere or under all circumstances. Imagine the democratization of a nation located in the middle of a deeply autocratic area. Its democratization would generate a number of autocratic-democratic dyads and thereby increase the risk of war. By contrast, the democratization of a nation surrounded by democracies would certainly be desirable. The democratic peace should be extended from its North Atlantic core area to contiguous areas first. Leapfrogging is undesirable. Geographical compactness of the democratic bloc might be a prerequisite for the pacifying effects of democracy to apply. Promoting democracy in Poland first and in Uzbekistan much later is not only more desirable, but also more feasible than the reverse order would be.

One recent challenge to my sketch of a capitalist peace implies the charge that I have been insufficiently enthusiastic about the impact of capitalism on peace while exaggerating the impact of democracy. In Gartzke's (2004) recent work, the pacifying impact of dyadic democracy and trade vanishes, once the effects of capital market integration are controlled. If Gartzke's findings were supported by future research, then the general idea that capitalism promotes peace would be strongly supported although two specific

---

18 Russett and Oneal (2001, p. 116) no longer accept this view. I doubt whether they are right. To me, results from a separate analysis of disputes in the Cold War period (Oneal and Russett 1997) look more persuasive than an analysis beginning in 1885 which collapses results from the multipolar pre-World War II period, the bipolar Cold War period and the beginning of the unipolar period thereafter. Some of the findings reported by Russett and Oneal (2001, p. 113), namely the qualitatively different alliance effects on militarized disputes found in the multipolar and bipolar periods of observation, cast doubt on the wisdom of imposing the same causal structure on different periods of world politics. In this respect, I find Gowa's (1999) approach quite reasonable.

arguments about **how** it pacifies might have to be modified or even eliminated. Both the pacifying effects of democracy and trade might be spurious, reflecting the common dependence of democracy, trade and avoidance of military conflict on capital market development and integration. In my view, however, it might be premature to discard the accumulated findings on pacifying democracy and trade effects in favor of a different and more radical version of capitalist peace theory which focuses on capital markets and their benefits for prosperity, democracy, and peace.

A standard objection against the efficacy of the capitalist peace points to World War I. It is frequently claimed that trade ties and economic interdependence between the entente and the Central European powers before World War I were strong. Should we therefore reject capitalist peace theory, or at least its 'peace by trade' component? In my view, such an evaluation would be premature and misleading. First, one has to remember that macropolitical propositions are probabilistic, not deterministic. Exceptions and anomalies are always to be expected. Of course, world wars are important anomalies. Before discussing the anomaly of the First World War in detail, however, I want to point out that the Second World War – which was even more deadly and worse than the first one – fits capitalist peace theory very well. Economic interdependence and trade between the future opponents of World War II was quite low. The allied democracies did not fight each other, but they fought one type of totalitarianism before they got into the Cold War with the other kind of totalitarianism. The pacifiers of capitalist peace theory were conspicuous by their absence before the worst war in human history.

Second, a closer look at World War I and its prehistory demonstrates that its exceptional character concerning capitalist peace theory should not be exaggerated. Although trade and economic interdependence between future war opponents were still high before World War I, the trend toward an ever more open global economy had already been arrested. As Lindsey (2002, p. 282, note 19) observed: "Until the 1870s, the clear trend had been toward progressive liberalization; afterwards, the overall trend was in the opposite direction. It was therefore plausible to extrapolate that barriers to trade would continue to grow, and indeed that extrapolation became the conventional wisdom throughout Europe. The simultaneous rush for colonies by all the major powers made for a convincing case that the emerging world order was one of rival autarchic blocs." Moreover, Lindsey (2002, p. 71) links the pessimistic expectations about the future of free trade to more general doubts about the viability of capitalism: "It was the expectation that countries would find it in their interest to close their economies to the outside world. And what created that expectation? It was the growing sense that national economic planning was the wave of the future."[19]

Lindsey's observations raise more questions than they answer. One conceivable way to proceed in future research might be to add a consideration of expectations of future trends to current trade – based, for example, on extrapolations. Another conceivable way might be to broaden the perspective from interstate trade to economic freedom in general. The only problem with this particular suggestion is that currently available economic freedom data do not extend back far enough to do it quickly. But one might remember that the main critic of 'peace by trade' (Barbieri 2002; Barbieri and Peters 2003) found a significant relationship between economic freedom and the avoidance of military conflict in the recent past. Another conceivable way might be to add ideological factors. The rise of Marxism – and even 'Kathedersozialismus' – may have undermined the hopes connected with capitalism and free trade. Operationalizing ideological currents in order to include them in quantitative studies, however, would be a daunting task which has not yet even begun. The point of these considerations has **not**

---

19 But the protectionism of the late 19th and early 20th century differed in kind from contemporary protectionism in the West. Today the main reason for high tariffs and other obstacles to free trade is some kind of misguided industrial policy, or the attempt to mitigate pressures for structural readjustment in the economy. Then, the dominant consideration was fiscal, that is, the desire to raise revenue for the state. If one imposes tariffs in order to raise revenue, of course, there are limits to the desirable height of tariffs. Otherwise, trade and tariff revenue might fall. By and large, protectionism before World War I was insufficient to reduce international trade (Hobson 1997, pp. 18, 188ff., 215; Lindsey 2002, p. 70). Nevertheless, growing obstacles to international trade should have resulted in expectations of worse to come, as has been argued by Lindsey (2002).

been to claim that World War I constitutes no empirical problem for the 'peace by trade' proposition, but merely to point out that a reconciliation of its occurrence and a modified capitalist peace theory is not to be ruled out.

Concerning trade before World War I, Russett and Oneal (2001, p. 175) themselves point out that "it had been dropping since a peak in 1906. Nor was it so great between most of the big 1914 adversaries... Germany's trade with France was much below that with Austria-Hungary and barely above that with the Netherlands, which had a much smaller economy than France's. French trade with Germany was only 75 percent of that with the United Kingdom and not much greater than with Belgium – a state far smaller than Germany. Austria-Hungary's biggest trading partner was its ally, Germany, which accounted for more than five times as much of its commerce as did France, Russia, or the United Kingdom. Of the six warring dyads (of major powers, E.W.), only two show high levels of interdependence. Russia and Britain were essentially tied as Germany's closest trading partners, while Germany was the largest trading partner of both Russia and, among the European states, Britain. But Britain's trade with the United States was about 40 percent greater than its trade with Germany..." This trading pattern could do little to pacify relations between Austria-Hungary and its great power opponents in World War I, and not much in the crucial Franco-German dyad. Without fighting in this dyad, it is hard to imagine as deadly a global war at the beginning of the 20th century as World War I became.

Third, the capitalist peace has to be put in perspective. In my own theoretical perspective which has been presented in the second section of this short book the motivation for war derives from security dilemmas and territorial conflicts. Both of these were present in Europe before 1914. Since the military balance between future opponents was **not** characterized by some pacifying overwhelming preponderance, war was possible. One out of two pacifiers of the capitalist peace, democracy, could hardly work. The prerogatives of monarchy were still too strong for Germany or Austria-Hungary being full democracies. Certainly, Russia remained an autocracy. If one insists on full adult suffrage as a defining characteristic of democracy, then even Britain became one only **after** World War I. Although economic interdependence and trade were high, they were not maximized where needed most for the sake of peace. They obviously did not suffice to pacify Europe at the beginning of the 20th century. The darkening horizon for international trade has already been pointed out above.[20]

Even if one insists that the First World War is incompatible with capitalist peace theory in spite of my 'excuses' above, one should note that there is little need for excuses there-

---

20 If one considers Russett and Oneal's (2001) 'Kantian peace' instead of my modification, 'the capitalist peace', then one should also mention that their third pacifier, a web of international organizations, was still quite weak. Before the great war there were few of them. The ones established thereafter could not prevent the carnage.

after: World War II, the Cold War[21] which became hot in Korea and Vietnam (and at risk of becoming so during the Cuban Missile Crisis), the Arab-Israeli wars, the Iraqi-Iranian War, the two American wars against Iraq, the Indo-Pakistani wars, the Sino-Indian War and the Taiwan Strait artillery duels were certainly not fought between democracies or champions of economic freedom engaged in much trade with each other. Thus, the biggest anomaly for capitalist peace theory – if it is one – happened a long time ago. Moreover, some quantitative studies even come close to modifying the 'peace by trade' proposition in such a way that one would expect anomalies to be more frequent in the remote than in the recent past. According to Hegre (2000), 'peace by trade' seems to work better at higher than at lower levels of economic development. Obviously, much of Europe was more highly developed after the 1960s than before 1914. According to Mousseau, Hegre, and Oneal (2003), it might be that the pacifying impact of democracy rather than the pacifying impact of trade (as previously suggested by Hegre, 2000) which depends on per capita incomes. Again, one would expect more anomalies for capitalist peace theory at the beginning of the 20th century rather than at its end.

---

21 One might argue that the Cold War is another anomaly because there has been only a cold war instead of a direct confrontation of Western and Warsaw Pact troops on the battlefield. In my view (Weede 1975, 1983), this can easily be explained by 'mutual assured destruction' and extended deterrence. There simply was no credible blueprint for victory in the nuclear age.

It may be argued that the different long-term effects of the settlements of the first and the second World War derive from failure or success to apply a capitalist peace strategy toward the losers of the war. After World War I, France determined the peace settlement more than anyone else. It failed to promote a capitalist peace. Reparations, inflation, immiseration and desperation within Germany contributed first to Hitler's empowerment and thereby to World War II in which France had to be saved by its allies. After World War II the United States pursued a capitalist peace strategy toward the vanquished. It succeeded in making allies out of Germany and Japan.

5. Capitalism, Democracy and the Avoidance of Domestic Conflict

Critics of globalization and the capitalist peace still may raise two serious 'objections'. First, the 'capitalist peace' – even if it exists – seems to address yesterday's problems rather than today's. According to Fearon and Laitin (2004, p. 6), "the main security threats and problems now emerge not from great power security competition – Russia and China, for example – but from the consequences of political disorder, misrule, and humiliation in the third world." While interstate war has become less frequent in the last decades, civil war has become the dominant form of military conflict (Gleditsch et al. 2002). Second, and worse still, it is sometimes argued that capitalism and the global integration of markets promotes inequality and poverty in less developed countries, and thereby reinforces the conflict-proneness of these countries. The first point, about the declining frequency of interstate war and the rising frequency of intrastate war, has to be granted as a statement of fact. But the wars of the twentieth century, including the two world wars, the Korean war, the Vietnam war, the Iraqi-Iranian war, the Arab-Israeli wars, the Indo-Pakistani wars and their casualties certainly demonstrated the persistent desirability of peace between states.

Moreover, the mere existence of weapons of mass destruction implies some warning that future wars might become even deadlier than the wars of the past. Since the means for generating an unprecedented disaster remain available, the avoidance of interstate war, especially of great power war, should remain a first-order priority. Nevertheless, it would be a tragedy, if capitalism and globalization would simultaneously reduce the risk of interstate war and increase the risk of intrastate war. Fortunately, the suspicion that economic freedom or capitalism promotes domestic conflict is **not** based on empirical research and findings. In bivariate analysis it seems that economic freedom is related to **less** domestic conflict and internal war.[22]

The theoretical basis of the suspected link between capitalism and rebellion is a simple causal chain where (1) capitalism or globalization – including free trade and foreign investment – lead to poverty or inequality in less developed countries, where (2) poverty and/or inequality lead to domestic upheavals, violence and civil war. Only if **both** links **were** empirically supported, there would be some reason to worry about the impact of capitalism and globalization on civil war and political instability.

---

22 Although there are numerous aspects of Tures' (2003) study which make me feel uncomfortable, one may reconstruct the relative frequencies of internal conflict in economically free, partly free, and non-free states and economies. These relative frequencies support his conclusion of a relationship between economic freedom and the avoidance of economic conflict or internal war.

First, I shall address the economic consequences of capitalism, free trade, and foreign direct investment in the current era of globalization. In my view, the economic freedom scales (Gwartney, Lawson, and Samida 2000; Gwartney and Lawson 2003, 2004; O'Driscoll, Holmes, and Kirkpatrick 2001) best assess how 'capitalist' economies are. The scales take into consideration how well property rights are protected by the rule of law, whether the state desists from confiscatory taxation, whether there is high and volatile inflation, how bad bureaucratic red tape and regulation are, and how protectionist the state is. Empirically, there is no doubt that economically free societies are richer than unfree societies.

Qualitative and historical studies (Jones 1981/1991, 1988; Landes 1998; North 1981, 1990; Pipes 1999; Weede 1996, 2000) support the temporal precedence of (relatively) safe property rights and (some degree of) economic freedom **before** the achievement of (relatively) high per capita incomes. In essence, it can be argued that economic development – or overcoming mass poverty – depends on some political prerequisites. The state **must not** be ruled by an exploitative upper class. Instead it should recognize and protect the private property rights of producers and traders. Instead it should facilitate commerce and widen markets by reducing transaction costs. Historically, this has happened in the West before it happened in the great Asian civilizations. It happened in Japan earlier than elsewhere in Asia.

Within the West, and to a lesser degree in Japan, too, the main reason why rulers started to respect the property rights of subjects – whether farmers, artisans, or merchants – has been political fragmentation. Wherever the market has been wider than the size of political units, economic actors may exercise exit options. Rulers who tax or confiscate more, or more arbitrarily, and who provide fewer services in the protection of property rights, resolution of disputes, or infrastructure have been likely to lose commerce and some of the most entrepreneurial of their subjects. In the long run, they weakened their economic base and their capabilities to raise armies and to defend themselves. So, the political fragmentation of Europe forced European rulers to become more benign than they would have been without interstate rivalry and to permit capitalism to grow.

But there is other evidence to link capitalism (or economic freedom) with human welfare. Most of the 48 studies which econometrically analyzed the impact of economic freedom on economic growth resulted in significant and positive effects, and only a single one reported a negative effect (Doucouliagos and Ulubasoglu 2004).[23] Although one may plausibly argue that positive findings fit better with the expectations of most economists, reviewers and editors of economic journals, I am not convinced that one should give too much weight to this consideration and therefore assume that published empirical work exaggerates the strength of the relationship between freedom and growth. Instead I suspect that these econometric studies tend to **underestimate** the impact of economic freedom on economic growth. Since all of these studies have to rely on data referring to the 1970s or later for reasons of data availability, these studies simply cannot adequately include the long-run economic damage which the absence of economic freedom has generated in centrally planned economies. All too often poorly performing Soviet-type economies were **not** included in econometric studies for lack of data. Moreover, one may argue that some or even most quantitative studies suffer from excessive controls for intervening variables. If one imagines that economic freedom is an ultimate source of growth, but that physical or human capital formation are proximate sources of growth, then controlling for such intervening variables must seriously weaken the relationship between economic freedom and growth. Therefore, I believe that the linkage between economic freedom and growth has usually been underestimated.

---

23   In the econometric literature it has been argued (de Haan and Siermann 1998; de Haan and Sturm 2000) that the relationship between improvements in economic freedom and growth looks more robust than the relationship between the level of freedom and growth. This finding, however, raises the issue of endogeneity. Moreover, Cole (2003) approached the issue of robustness differently by analyzing the impact of economic freedom and its improvement in two quite different growth models. In his analysis, the impact of the level of economic freedom on growth rates has been stronger than the impact of improvements in economic freedom. In Gwartney and Lawson's (2004, p. 41) analysis, both level and change effects of freedom on growth look fairly strong.

In qualitative pair comparisons, however, one can easily look at more or less capitalist and Soviet-type economies. Elsewhere (Weede 2001/2002) I compared the economic performance of Russia and South Korea in the 20th century. Although Russia was a great power at the beginning of the 20th century when Korea became a Japanese colony, although the (Russian dominated) Soviet Union could challenge even the United States in the 1950s when Korea was devastated by a war, although Korea ca. 2000 had about one hundred million less people than (post-Soviet) Russia, the South Korean economy then approximately equaled the Russian one in size which implies a per capita income of about three or four times as high in South Korea as in Russia. Or, if one compares Mainland China and Russia (or the Soviet Union) since the late 1970s, the results are equally dramatic. Then Russia's per capita income was about 16 times as high as Chinese incomes, by the turn of the century and millennium the gap was down to 2 to 1 or less (Weede 2002). The dramatic Chinese improvement can be explained by reference to earlier capitalist reforms in China than in Russia, by a Chinese focus on agricultural reforms at first in contrast to persistent Russian delays in reforming agriculture, and by a much more open and export-oriented economy in China than in Russia.

Concerning the impact of economic freedom on size distributions of income, there are few studies. But Gwartney, Lawson, and Samida (2000, p. 17) and Mehlkop (2002) found no significant relationship. By and large, this is good news for the poor. If economic freedom or capitalism tend to produce prosperity and growth without any regressive distributional impact, then the poor benefit from it. The benefits of capitalism to the poor can be documented in different ways. Gwartney, Lawson and Samida (2000, p. 16) as well as Mehlkop (2002) looked at life expectancy and found that it was much better in economically free societies than elsewhere. Obviously, long life expectancies can only be achieved, where all classes benefit from it – including the numerous poor in less developed societies. This advantage of economically free societies in life expectancy remains true even where per capita income differences have been controlled.

Dollar and Kraay (2002) used a very different approach and asked whether and to which degree the poor participate in higher average incomes within their nation. By and large, there is something close to a one-to-one relationship. If average incomes go up by a dollar, then the incomes of the poor go up by a similar amount of money. Although globalization-induced growth admittedly does little benefit to those countries which do **not** participate in globalization – much of Africa does not – globalization certainly has improved the lot of hundreds of millions Chinese and increasingly does so with Indians, too. According to the Indian economist Bhalla (2002), economic growth in the era of globalization has already reduced global inequality between persons and households because populous Asian countries, in particular China and India and their inhabitants, benefited so much. Collier and

Dollar (2002), the Economist (2004a), Ravaillon (2004), and Wolf (2004, chapter 9) produced or discussed other and somewhat less optimistic evaluations of trends in income distributions and poverty elimination, but all of them underline that progress in Asia – where most of mankind lives – is undeniable.[24]

On top of the more general studies of the impact of capitalism and/or globalization there are lots of other studies which demonstrated that economic openness, free trade, and export orientation help poor countries to outgrow poverty (Bleany and Nishiyama 2002; Dollar 1992; Edwards 1998; Lindert and Williamson 2001, p. 37; Sachs and Warner 1997). Finally, there are empirical studies which demonstrate a positive impact of foreign direct investment on economic growth (de Soysa and Oneal 1999; de Soysa 2003; OECD 1998). Actually, a dollar of foreign investment is much more productive than a dollar of domestic investment is in poor countries.

Taken together these stylized facts produced by the literature on the effects of capitalism or economic freedom, free trade and foreign direct investment in the current era of glob-

---

24 Undoubtedly, Africa is a black spot. But since it hardly is economically free, since it does not significantly participate in global markets, one should not blame capitalism for the African predicament. As the Economist (2004a, p. 75) recently observed: "Sub-Saharan Africa suffers not from globalisation, but from lack of it."

alization imply that capitalism and globalization, free trade and foreign investment are good for growth and good for the poor, for their life expectancy as well as for their consumption opportunities. Although economic freedom or capitalism and globalization do not overcome income inequality, one should no longer argue that they make it worse. Moreover, it has to be remembered that even persistent inequality becomes less harmful, if the poor participate in the fruits of growth, as they do under capitalism.

How detrimental the opposite of economic freedom or capitalism can be is best illustrated by the worst episode of mass starvation in the 20th century. In the late 1950s, Mao Zedong ruled China. He and his politbureau decided to dilute the property rights of the already collectivized Chinese peasantry even further. Before the so-called 'great leap forward', many farming collectives in China consisted of a single village. Many of these villages were dominated by a small number of extended families, or even a single one. Within such a context Chinese peasants were used to some degree of sharing the fruits of their labor. The 'great leap forward' essentially consisted of three steps. First, the older farming collectives were combined to huge multi-village 'people's communes'. This in itself diluted property rights and made consumption opportunities ever less dependent on one's own work effort. Second, the communes were encouraged to industrialize and to approximate autarchy. Like environmental enthusiasts of localism and self-sufficiency today, Mao forgot that subsistence economies cannot benefit from the division of labor (Wolf 2004, pp. 196-199). Third, agricultural decisions were made by commune leaderships who needed the trust and political protection of their superiors, but who did not necessarily know as much about local agriculture as even illiterate peasants know by experience.

The political constraints on economic freedom had achieved 'perfection'. For the time being, capitalism was overcome. The insights of Adam Smith (1776/1976/1990) and 18th century economics about the essential role of incentives provided by private property were disregarded. The insights of Hayek (1945, 1960/1971) about the impossibility of using the dispersed knowledge of millions of producers, including illiterate peasants, under central planning were disregarded, too. Thirty million people or more perished from starvation (Fu 1993, pp. 235, 304; Kristof and WuDunn 1994, p. 66; Sandschneider 1998, p. 173). By contrast, once China changed from communism under Mao to what I call 'creeping capitalism' under Deng Xiaoping, the economy improved dramatically. Hundreds of millions of people were relieved from severe poverty. In a quarter century income per head multiplied by a factor of seven (The Economist 2004d, p. 11).

In sum, there is **no** good reason to believe that capitalism or globalization, free trade or foreign investment harm less developed countries or their poorest classes. Quite to the contrary. Even if inequality or poverty **were** root causes of rebellion, political violence and civil war, overcoming capitalism and globalization, free trade and foreign investment would not be helpful. But, possibly, widely held views on the sources of violence and civil war lack empirical foundation, too. This is the problem to be addressed now.

Although much finer distinctions between research programs or theories of rebellion are possible and meaningful (see Rule 1988), I shall focus on a simple distinction. Rebellion, i.e., the use of violence against the authorities, may either be explained by discontent, grievances, relative deprivation or frustration (for example, Gurr 1968, 1970, 1980) or by expected utilities and likelihood to succeed, i.e., by rational choice (for example, Oberschall 1997; Tullock 1974). Of course, it is possible or even inevitable to combine both approaches. In my view, however, it makes sense to find out which approach is more successful if taken in isolation. At first, we need to know what matters most of all. Although the historical sociologist Skocpol (1976, p. 181) does not identify herself with the rational choice approach, she expressed one of its major insights very well: "Not oppression, but weakness breeds revolution. It is the breakdown of a societal mode of social control which allows and prompts social revolutions to unfold."

In principle, the deprivation approach seems fit to explain mass rebellions, i.e., violence by the miserable or poor, by the victims of discrimination or exploitation. A characteristic of the poor and exploited, however, is that they individually do not control significant resources. If a poor individual joins a rebellion, he or she is unlikely to tip the balance of power against an exploitative and repressive government. According to the 'logic of collective action' (Olson 1965/1968), a rational and selfish cost-benefit calculation must lead to the conclusion that it is better to do nothing, to let others try to improve society. If better government or a 'just' society is a public good – for example, if 'justice' is understood in egalitarian rather than hierarchical or meritocratic terms – then non-contributors cannot easily be excluded without endangering an egalitarian conception of justice, then freeriding is rational. Even keeping the probabilistic nature of macropolitical theorizing in mind, there is a fundamental difference between deprivation approaches and rational choice. Deprivation theorists should expect mass rebellions to be fairly frequent, rational choice theorists expect them to be extremely rare. This raises the question of a standard of comparison against which 'frequent' and 'rare' are to be judged.

If people are selfish and rational, then one should expect those to rebel who stand a chance to succeed because they already control significant resources. Although wealth may be useful, the most immediately useful resource is control over guns. Whoever controls a loyal tank division, preferably close to the capital, or a loyal regiment of paratroopers obviously stands a chance of making a difference, of tilting the balance of power against the government or of defending the government against rebels. Since colonels or other officers of coup-prone ranks are not yet presidents, it is easier for them to imagine lavish rewards or advancement in case of successful rebellion than in case of loyal defense of the previous government. So, the standard of comparison in evaluating the frequency of mass rebellions is the frequency of elite rebellions, in particular of military coups d'état.

Such a comparison is not easy because quantitative data, even mere enumerations or lists of mass rebellions were not widely used and recognized as valid until recently.[25] Although the situation is much better for coups d'état, the reliability of the ratio depends on the quality of both numbers. Working with different data sets and assumptions, Weede and Muller (1998, p. 48) provide some educated guesses of what the true ratio **might** look like. In one of their estimates the number of coups is about 15 times as high as the number of rebellions, in the other one it is about 25 times as high. This looks like a difference in order of magnitude. Only a rational choice approach can explain why coups are so much more frequent than mass rebellions.

Of course, one may **describe** any conceivable finding on relative frequencies in relative deprivation terms. Then one would ascribe feelings of relative deprivation to all those colonels who have not yet been president. The problem with such an ascription is not necessarily that it implies a wrong

---

25   Recently, an operational definition of civil war seems to prevail according to which rebel military challenges must have resulted in at least 1000 combat-related deaths before the event is counted as a civil war (Collier et al. 2003). A new compilation of conflict data including civil wars (Gleditsch et al. 2002) permits the application of multiple thresholds of conflict severity.

description of the feelings of coup-makers but that it has no other falsifiable implication than a prohibition of presidents organizing coups against themselves. Everyone below the president might feel deprived. From a rational choice perspective, feelings of deprivation might be too widely held to distinguish between likely rebels and others, whereas control over resources, especially over military resources, is sufficiently concentrated to permit predictions about who is likely to rebel and to succeed.[26]

Actually, rational choice theory (Tullock 1974) provides an argument of why the fruits of violent rebellion turn out to be so ghastly. Consider the cost-benefit calculations of ordinary citizens in a civil war, in a violent contest between government and rebels. Being resource-poor, **ordinary** citizens are unlikely to affect the outcome of the contest. If they are rational and motivated by the consequences of their actions for themselves, they disregard what they cannot affect in any case. Instead ordinary citizens or subjects pursue private aims, like staying alive, or avoiding torture, imprisonment and starvation. If one side in the contest kills and tortures its

---

26 It is hard to argue that rebellions or revolutions, i. e., successful rebellions resulting in structural change, have achieved much for the people, whether in terms of prosperity or in terms of liberty (Weede and Muller 1997). A rational choice approach to rebellion and revolution easily can accommodate the so-called 'iron law of oligarchy' (Michels 1910/1970) which permits individuals advocating egalitarianism to win power, but prohibits egalitarianism ever to be practiced. Rule by Communist politbureaus perfectly illustrates the point.

opponents or people whom it suspects to be opponents at will, while the other side tends to respect moral or legal rules, it is much safer to be suspected of sympathies for the more cruel side than being suspected of sympathies for the less cruel side. Intimidation by cruelty is likely to help the most ruthless side to win a civil war. If cruelty and ruthlessness have helped rebels to grab political power, it is hard to see why victors should give up exactly those habits which have served them so well. The theoretical implication of a rational choice approach is clear. Violent rebellion and revolution should more frequently lead to **less** humane government than existed before the rebellion than to improvements in the humanitarian record of government. Even a superficial look at Communists, or Muslim rebels taking power in Iran or Afghanistan, illustrates the point quite well.

The previous section of this paper, on war, mostly referred to regression type analyses. This section, on rebellion and civil war, essentially relied on qualitative or 'order of magnitude'-differences in defending the primacy of a rational choice over a relative deprivation approach. Elsewhere (Weede 1998), I reviewed cross-national studies on rebellion and civil war and found little **robust** support for a relative deprivation approach. There is a small, but growing number of cross-national studies which address propositions derived from a rational choice perspective. A finding from cross-national studies that fits a rational choice approach well is the linkage between certain types of **rich** natural resource endowments and proneness to rebellion, violence and civil war. Diamonds are an extreme case of a resource which is easily alienable, hidden, transported and, ultimately, sold for private gain as well as for financing rebellions. One should expect rational actors, i.e., greedy utility maximizers, to exploit such opportunities. They do it at the expense of the civilian population. Resource wealth (for example, oil, minerals, gem stones, and drugs) does make civil war more likely, longer, and more deadly (Ross 2004). Rapacity drives civil wars more than paucity does (de Soysa 2000; 2002; de Soysa and Wagner 2003).[27]

Equally important, although less obviously related to the validity of the rational choice approach is another finding of the same work: Open economies are less prone to civil violence than closed economies (also confirmed by Hegre, Gissinger and Gleditsch 2003; Tures 2003). Economic openness might be an antidote to war **and** civil violence. This finding is directly relevant to the above discussed concern whether the capitalist peace between states may be bought at the expense of more civil wars. This is **not** the case. Moreover, economic openness, interdependence, and trade seem to promote democratization, at least under certain circumstances (Rogowski 1990).

---

[27] But in contrast to some theoretical expectations, it has not been supported that "nascent rebel groups ... gained funding before the war broke out from the extraction or sale of natural resources" (Ross 2004, p. 50).

Another relevant cross-national finding is the non-monotonic relationship between regime repressiveness on the one hand and violence on the other hand. Muller and Weede (1990, p. 646) made the following argument in explaining it: "The hypothesis of an inverted U-curve between institutionalized repressiveness and political violence is based on the assumption that the structure of the regime constrains or facilitates political behavior of individuals by affecting opportunities for peaceful and violent collective action, the expected probability of success in each kind of action and the expected costs of each. Under a highly repressive regime it is likely that opportunities for collective political action of any type will be low, that the probability of success will be negligible, and that costs will be high. Rational actors who wish to contest the policies of a government are likely to think better of it. Under a non-repressive regime, it is likely that opportunities for collective political action of any kind will be high, that the probability of success of peaceful collective action will typically be much higher than that of violence, and that the costs of peaceful collective action will be much lower than those of violence. Rational actors therefore are likely to prefer peaceful collective action to violence. Under a semi-repressive regime, it is likely that opportunities for collective action will be available to some extent, that the probability of success of peaceful collective action typically will be negligible, and that violent action therefore may be preferred."

Since the period of violence analyzed by Muller and Weede was very short (1973–77), it is reassuring that a group of Norwegian researchers (Hegre, Ellingsen, Gates and Gleditsch 2001, p. 44) did arrive at the same conclusion on the special conflict-proneness of semi-repressive or, as they say, "intermediate" regimes. Since their time frame spans the entire 1816–1992 period, we can be confident that the earlier finding was no short-lived aberration from usual historical patterns. These findings, however, point **not only** to a democratic domestic peace, but also to an autocratic domestic peace. Moreover, the Norwegians found out that democracies tend to be more stable and concluded their analysis with these words: "While totalitarian states may achieve a domestic peace of sorts... a democratic civil peace is likely not only to be more just but also more durable." Moreover, even if autocratic or totalitarian states were as effective as democracies in preventing political upheaval and domestic violence, democracy and trade openness significantly reduce the risk that governments (or occasionally some other civil war contender) resort to genocide or politicocide and other human rights violations (Harff 2003; Harrelson-Stephens and Callaway 2003).

By now, there is quite solid evidence that poor countries are much more afflicted with rebellion and violence than rich countries are (Collier et al. 2003; Fearon and Laitin 2003; Hegre 2003; Henderson and Singer 2000). There seems to be a direct pacifying impact of prosperity. On top of this, there is an indirect pacifying impact of prosperity via democracy because richer countries are more likely to be democratic (Lipset 1994), and because democratic countries are more likely to enjoy civil peace than semi-repressive regimes.

At first glance, it looks as if the finding about poverty and domestic conflict fitted a relative deprivation approach to violence better than a rational choice approach. In poor countries more people are deprived than in rich countries. Such an interpretation would gain credibility, if quantitative research had also found that income inequality contributes to violence. Although there exist studies to make this point, other work serves to raise strong objections or to negate or, at least, to severely qualify such a statement (Fearon and Laitin 2004, p. 22; Hegre, Gissinger and Gleditsch 2003; Muller 1985; Muller und Weede 1993; Weede 1986). Recently, the World Bank (Collier et al. 2003, pp. 66, 80) has argued that inequality does not affect the risk of conflict, but its duration. The empirical basis for the latter effect, however, must be tenuous because of the limited variation between countries suffering from civil war. Moreover, most of these countries are poor and autocratic. Their income distribution data are likely to be among the least reliable ones. – Moreover, one also may regard high per capita incomes as a proxy for state strength. Because of its correlation with state weakness and failure, poverty might indicate opportunities for rebellion. The association between poverty and civil war might be expected because of cost benefit calculations (Fearon and Laitin 2003). So, whether this correlation provides more comfort for rational choice or deprivation theorists is not at all clear.

6. Why We Need the Capitalist Peace, and Why We Can Afford It

It has been argued above that the two major sources of interstate war are the security dilemma and territorial conflicts. Both may lead to dissatisfaction with the status quo. In the nuclear age, extended deterrence and 'peace through fear' may neutralize otherwise irreconcilable conflicts of interest. The timing of military challenges to the status quo depends on power balances. The rise of revisionist powers, the decline of satisfied status quo powers, and approximate parity between rival and strategically interdependent nations is most dangerous.[28] Hegemony or unipolarity overcomes, or at least mitigates, anarchy and thereby contributes to the avoidance of war, i.e., hegemony reduces the likelihood and severity of military challenges to the status quo. The end of the cold war, the dissolution of the Warsaw Pact and the

---

28 Obviously, it makes little sense to speak of a power balance between Peru and Hungary, or even between Japan and Saudi Arabia. These nations are not strategically interdependent, although Japan and Saudi Arabia are economically interdependent. In empirical studies, strategic interdependence is frequently assessed by either contiguity or by at least one state in a pair of states being a great power.

Soviet Union resulted in unipolarity. No one is capable of challenging the United States in the next decades. Currently, the US spends as much on the military as the next 15 to 20 biggest spenders combined (Brooks and Wolforth 2002). Whereas the avoidance of major wars during the Cold War period rested on fear of 'mutual assured destruction' and extended deterrence (Weede 1983; 1996, chapter 7), now it rests on American supremacy. Since nuclear deterrence may fail because of accidents or miscalculation, supremacy is much safer than nuclear deterrence ever could be.

Given a mixture of creeping disarmament and disunity in Europe as well as a rather poor economic performance in Japan and most of Continental Europe since the 1990s, given the demographic decline of Europe and Japan, no rich nation or bloc of rich nations is likely to develop the capability to challenge the US in the foreseeable future. Moreover, even a more powerful Europe or a more powerful Japan would be unlikely challengers even to a declining United States. Democracy, trade and cooperation in intergovernmental organizations provide sufficiently strong links to pacify the zone of peace including America, Europe and Japan. Russia is no longer a credible challenger. Its economic base is simply too weak. Russia is in demographic decline, too. Its economy is comparable in size to Los Angeles County or South Korea, but not to the United States (The Economist 2004c, p.4; Weede 2001-2002). Even Russia's weapons of mass destruction will become obsolete over time.

Given current economic trends conceivable challenges to American hegemony can only come from Asia. The growing importance of Asia in the world economy is best illustrated by the composition of the global middle class which may be defined by a daily income per person between ten and forty US-dollar in 1993 purchase power parity terms. According to Bhalla (2002, p. 187), "in 1960, 6 percent of the world's middle-class population came from Asia; today, that share is 52 percent. If the world's middle class was basically white in 1960 (industrialized-world residents constituted 63 percent), today it is basically Asian." Within Asia, of course, its demographic giants, China and India, play a special role.

The most plausible challenger to the United States on the horizon is Mainland China. Using purchase power parity data (World Bank 2003, pp. 252–253), the economic size of China (including Hong Kong) is about 57 % of America's size. In another decade, ca. 2015, the Chinese economy might be as large as the Amercan one (Maddison 1998, pp. 17, 96). Of course, there will remain a huge gap in per capita incomes. As an autocracy, however, China is capable of allocating a larger share of its resources to the military than a democracy can (Payne 1989). From a capability point of view, China **might** become a rising challenger. Moreover, a rising China can easily find reasons to be dissatisfied. The United States still supports and arms Taiwan which Mainland China regards as a renegade province.

But there are reasons for hope, too. The rapidity of the rise of China not only provides the resources for a challenge. It simultaneously establishes the precondition for sustainable democracy. If China should attempt democratic reforms[29], economic performance might make them viable and sustainable in a decade or so. South Korea and Taiwan have already demonstrated the compatibility of a Confucian political culture and successful democratization. Although the democratic peace does **not yet** apply to China and the West, other components of the capitalist peace already exert some beneficial influence. At the end of the 20th century, China may have exported between 30 % and 44 % of its gross domestic product at market prices (Noland, Liu, Robinson and Wang 1998, p. 58; Wolf 2004, p. 144). Over one third of these exports have gone to America (Lampton 2003, p. 41). Moreover, trade is not the only tie that binds the American and Chinese economies together. There is a lot of American direct investment in China.[30] There are huge Chinese purchases of US government securities (Quinlan 2002). Economic interdependence between China on the one hand and America or the West on the other hand should already exert some pacifying impact. Moreover, cooperation in intergovernmental organizations also increases. China's

---

29 Elections at the village level (Rowen 1996) and the training of an increasing number of lawyers (Pei 1998) are encouraging events.

30 Since foreign-funded enterprises account for the lion's share of China's exports, it has even been argued that China "has joined the global economy on terms that reinforce its dependence on foreign technology and investment and restrict its ability to become an industrial and technological threat to advanced industrial democracies" (Gilboy 2004, p. 34).

recent accession to the World Trade Organization symbolizes this trend.

As Taiwan is the most likely bone of contention between the United States and Mainland China, relations between both Chinese states matter, too. Trade and economic cooperation across the Taiwan Strait become ever more important. Taiwan-based enterprises have invested in between 70 and 100 billion US-$ on the Mainland. About one third of Taiwanese exports go to the Mainland, including Hong Kong. More than one million people from Taiwan are estimated to work on the Mainland (Finsterbusch 2003). Thus, trade and economic cooperation between Mainland China on the one hand and Taiwan or the US on the other hand, even creeping economic integration between the Mainland and Taiwan, provide the strongest reason for optimism about future relations between China and the West.

Finally, the growing and vigorous economic and organizational ties between China and the West seem to strengthen the prospects for democratization. Receiving foreign direct investment, as China does, is related to better prospects for democratization (de Soysa 2003). China's attempts to make itself an attractive destination for foreign investment already exerts some beneficial effects on its domestic property rights. As recently recognized by Gallagher (2002, p. 359): "laws that were adopted for the whole economy were largely based on the laws already written for foreign-invested firms." Similarly, Wolf (2004, p. 276) argues that WTO

(World Trade Organization) "membership is an effective way of importing the rule of law." Strengthening private property rights might in the long run be more useful to democratization than the rapid introduction of elections, as Zakaria (2003) recently argued in comparing Russia and China. Although China does not yet enjoy the rule of law, some of its preconditions are established. In the last quarter century, the number of lawyers multiplied by a factor of sixty. Two judges on China's highest court got some of their training at Harvard or Yale. Moreover, the Chinese government seems to be losing more lawsuits than it is winning (Economy 2004, p. 101). So, the big picture – referring to great and rising powers – provides some reasons for hope based on economic freedom, capitalism, free trade and their consequences for prosperity, democracy and peace.

The black clouds on the horizon derive from two concerns. First, there might be a resurgence of protectionism in rich countries. Western democracies might no longer wish to stand the reinforcement of 'creative destruction' by global competition. The recent failure of trade negotiations in Cancun (September 2003) does illustrate this danger.[31] Worst of all, China-bashing seems to become popular in the United States. In late 2003, the United States took unilateral safeguard action against some Chinese textile and clothing exports (Economist 2003b). Although this action has been legal, from a capitalist peace point of view it looks unwise. Second, globalization helps the globalizers only (Bhalla 2002; Collier and Dollar 2002; Dollar and Kraay 2002). Sub-saharan Africa and big parts of the Muslim world barely participate. They remain mired in poverty, stagnation and civil war. As long as they do, they remain beyond the reach of the capitalist peace, too.

Since September 11, 2001, terrorism emanating from the Muslim world is a special security concern. Although I do not want to belittle the suffering of the victims of the attack on the twin towers of the World Trade Center in New York or the Pentagon in Washington, the event should be kept in perspective. The number of people suffering because of al-Qaeda is not comparable to the numbers suffering in the World Wars, the Korean and Vietnam wars, or the trench warfare between Iraq and Iran in the 1980s. It is not comparable to the mass murders inflicted by the Communists or Nazis. It seems best comparable to the persistent suffering from Palestinian terrorism in Israel. At worst, al-Qaeda can hope 'to succeed' in killing or maiming a similar share of the

---

31 Another illustration comes from a recent econometric study. According to Mueller and Stratmann (2003), democratic participation is associated with a more equal distribution of income, larger government sectors and therefore slower economic growth rates. The attempt to achieve social justice within rich countries by redistribution might interfere with Western countries providing models for emulation to less developed countries as well as with the provision of open markets for LDC products. – It also bears repetition, however, to point out that poor countries tend to be more protectionist than rich countries. Whereas agricultural tariffs in the US average 12 %, in Brazil the percentage is 37, and in India 112 (Bhagwati 2004a, p. 59).

population in America or the West as Palestinian terrorists have done in Israel. Israel does survive and so would America and the West in what I believe to be the worst case scenario – that is, even if the worst deeds of terrorism are still ahead of us rather than behind us.

America and the West are far too strong economically and militarily to risk losing against an economically stagnant and politically disunited realm of Islam or a tiny terrorist minority recruited among Muslims. But al-Qaeda, like-minded and affiliated terrorist organizations might be strong enough to isolate the realm of Islam, to drive away most tourists, many traders, and most foreign investors. Al-Qaeda might 'succeed' in preventing the Arabs or even the wider Muslim world from participating in globalization and its benefits. By and large, growth and globalization have been good for the poor, raising average incomes, and the incomes of the poor, and mitigating global inequality among persons and households (Bhalla, 2002; Collier and Dollar 2002). Al-Qaeda's success might be to keep Arabs, or even the wider Muslim community, poor and 'pure', i. e., protected from the lure of Western, secularist or un-Islamic ways of life. Although there might be some form of Western presence at the oil wells, an al-Qaeda success could condemn Arab or Muslim civilization to fall ever farther behind the West and behind the rest of the world – economically, technologically, and scientifically. A persistently poor Arab or Muslim civilization would remain non-democratic and could participate neither in the democratic nor in the wider capitalist peace. Only Arabs or Muslims, however, can avoid this fate of their civilization. The West might well be condemned to having to wait until Muslims themselves recognize that al-Qaeda offers them nothing better than hostility and isolation, continued poverty and stagnation.

Nevertheless, the contemporary combination of the capitalist peace by globalization and American hegemony promotes the avoidance of war, especially of major power war. Unipolar or hegemonic international systems are less war-prone than others.[32] Since the US is the only surviving superpower, we benefit from living in such a system. No replacement for the US is on the horizon, certainly not the European Union. Demography, a legacy of inefficient state interference with the economy, and persistent quarreling and disunity within Europe suffice to prevent the rise of Europe even to great power status. Therefore, the end of American hegemony might also threaten ideas and ideals invented in the West, including the rule of law and economic freedom, capitalism and democracy. If a libertarian China or India ever came into existence, if one of these states were ready for global leadership at the end of the 21st century, no proponent of freedom should object. Currently, however, political liberty and economic freedom have an insufficient toehold on Mainland Asia. That is why no desirable substitute for

---

32 One might add that short wars are a lesser evil than protracted wears. Since the end of the Cold War, the US has won its wars within short periods of time.

American leadership is yet conceivable. Ultimately, the prospect of a capitalist peace has been and still is underwritten and promoted by American power and dominance.[33]

---

33 See Gowa (1994). – There is some similarity between my view and Lal's (2003). Most of all I agree with his warnings against American attempts to legislate 'habits of the heart' and against ethical imperialism. Like Lal, I think that economic liberalism (or libertarianism) and foreign policy realism should be reconciled. – Ultimately, the question is whether the promotion of capitalism and democracy will ever suffice to overcome the war-promoting temptations arising out of military equivalence. But a cure which sometimes works is better than none at all.

7. What Must be Done to Promote the Capitalist Peace

Rummel (1994) has pointed out that autocracy has killed even more people than interstate war or rebellion or revolution in the 20th century. Even if an autocratic peace within or between nations should exist – in spite of studies (Fearon and Laitin 2003, p. 85; Peceny, Beer, and Sanchez-Terry 2002) which call these claims into question – the autocratic cure looks even bloodier than the diseases of war and civil war.[34] Therefore, the preservation of democracy where it already exists and democratization elsewhere must be part of the solution to the problems of rebellion, political violence and war. Since the empirical studies discussed above have demonstrated some fairly strong effects of democracy on the avoidance of war **between democracies,** since democracies are less afflicted with rebellion and civil war (Muller and Weede 1990; Hegre et al. 2001), democracy and democratization constitute instruments to mitigate political

---

34 Harff (2003), like Rummel (1994), has documented the relationship between autocracy and politicocide, i.e., mass murder for political reasons. But her data base covers only the period since 1955.

violence. This raises the question of what can be done to promote and underwrite democracy.

According to Lipset (1994) or Boix and Stokes (2003), the viability of democratic regimes and the likelihood of transitions to democracy rest upon the level of economic development. The more prosperous a country is, the more likely it is to become and to remain a democracy. Since this proposition has been strongly supported by cross-national studies, and much better than any other conceivable determinant or precondition of democracy, one may argue that the promotion of democracy necessitates providing a helping hand to poor countries. This can be done in different ways.

First, prosperous countries influence the legal foundations for capitalism or economic policies elsewhere. How much this matters has been demonstrated by the divided nations during the cold war period where one part was influenced by the Soviet Union, and the other part by the United States. Economies benefiting from American influence, like West Germany, South Korea and Taiwan, did much better than East Germany, North Korea or Mainland China which were inspired by the Soviet model. Since China gave up socialist practices and converted to creeping capitalism in the late 1970s, it multiplied per capita incomes by a factor of seven (Economist 2004d) and almost closed a 16 to 1 gap in per capita incomes with Russia (Weede 2002). The idea of advice should not be too narrowly conceived. By providing a model for emulation, successful countries **implicitly** provide advice to others. In general terms, the best institutional and policy advice may be summarized by "promote economic freedom" (Berggren 2003; Kasper 2004).[35] Cross-national studies (Cole 2003; Dollar 1992; Edwards 1998; Farr, Lord, and Wolfenbarger 1998; de Haan and Sierman 1998; de Haan and Sturm 2000; Gwartney and Lawson 2004, chapter 2; Vega-Gordillo and Alvarez-Arce 2003; Weede and Kämpf 2002) tend to demonstrate that economic freedom **or** improvements in economic freedom increase growth rates. Together with property rights protected by the rule of law, the absence of confiscatory taxation, the avoidance of high and volatile inflation, the avoidance of too much bureaucratic red tape and regulation, economic openness or export orientation is part of the package of economic freedom.

An essential part of the economic freedom package is the limitation of the scope of politics. As Wolf (2004, p. 30) has observed, such a limitation may be another prerequisite of democracy: "A political entity (be it an individual, family or

---

35 A less 'libertarian' or 'Hayekian' policy advice might be "promote market-enhancing governance structures", that is accountability, participation, predictability, and transparency. Although "getting interventions right" (Ahrens 2002, p. 217) is not necessarily empty advice, it certainly is more difficult advice to follow than "promote economic freedom". Moreover, there is some overlap in the two types of advice, for example, in the recommendation of competition, export promotion, honest administration, open markets, and the rule of law.

party) that controls all a country's resources, through a state, is unlikely to allow any opposition access to the means of campaigning against it. Worse, if all economic decisions are political, loss of power threatens a loss of livelihood. Power becomes the only route to wealth. This is not just lethal for the economy. It is also lethal for democratic politics which becomes a form of civil war. It is only when politics are not a matter of personal survival that a stable democracy is conceivable. For a democracy to function, therefore, the domain of the political has to be circumscribed. The market economy, based on private property, achieves this."

As Deng Xiaoping has demonstrated in Mainland China, changes towards economic freedom need not wait for democratization. Nor do they need to approach perfection in order to be effective in stimulating economic growth. Few observers credit China with anything like the rule of law. By devolving much economic decision-making to provinces, counties, and cities, however, China may have established some 'market-preserving federalism' (Weingast 1995) and thereby something of a partial functional substitute for the rule of law. In order to carry favor with foreign investors, including overseas Chinese investors, regional and local governments have to act **as if** they desired to respect private property rights, to generate **some** degree of predictability in public administration and to improve infrastructure. Certainly, small, tentative, and regionally limited steps toward economic freedom are better than none. They may serve as first steps in a transformation towards capitalism.

Second, prosperous and democratic countries may provide open markets for exports from poor countries. Without a fairly open American market neither Western Europe nor Japan would have overcome the terrible legacy of World War II as quickly as they did. Without a fairly open American market, the East Asian economic miracles might never have happened. South Korea and Taiwan might still be poor and ruled by autocrats instead of being fairly prosperous and democratic. Unfortunately, rich Western societies in general, and welfare states in particular, find it hard to provide an open door to poor country exports. Take sugar and the European Union as an example. Production costs are six times as high in the European Union as in Brazil. Nevertheless, the European Union prefers to subsidize sugar production at home to importing it from Brazil, Malawi, Zambia, or Thailand. As the Economist (2004b, p. 73) recently wrote, this is "economically stupid" and it is "morally indefensible". Unfortunately, it is also politics as usual.

Moreover, rich and democratic countries may promote a universal and multilateral trading system with a dispute settlement mechanism instead of a hodgepodge of bilateral and regional free trade agreements which easily degenerates into trade diversion and trade bloc rivalry. Since small countries are more trade dependent than big ones, such a multilateral system is even more important for them than for the big powers. As Wolf (2004, p. 91) has observed, there is another reason why less developed and poorly governed countries need an international trade regime more than well governed countries: "The countries that gain the most from strong and enforceable international agreements are weak ones with poor reputations. They gain from the constraints on the actions of stronger partners. But they so gain from the acceptance of constraints on their own behavior (as do all members), which make their liberal intentions towards trade and investment more credible. Ulysses, too, saw the value of binding himself to the mast. Constraints on sovereignty are, therefore, the aim of the exercise. In a world of international transactions and multiple jurisdictions, constraints on sovereignty are also desirable. Otherwise, the potential for conflict and unpredictability seems almost limitless."

Third, rich and democratic countries might provide much more foreign direct investment (FDI) to poor countries than they do. Even the nominally still Communist regime in the People's Republic of China welcomes FDI. Since China is capable of internal financing of its investments, it illustrates well why poor countries should promote FDI irrespective of their capital needs. As Wolf (2004, p. 263) has argued, "the inflow of foreign direct investment matters...as a way of accelerating the transfer of know-how..." Foreign direct investment not only promotes growth and prosperity even more vigorously than domestic investment does, but it also directly promotes democratization (de Soysa and Oneal 1999; de Soysa 2003; Burkhart and de Soysa 2002). Since the US current account deficit more than balances European and Japanese surpluses, the high income countries, collectively, tend to be net importers of capital at the beginning of the 21st century (Wolf 2004, p. 114). Bigger capital flows from rich to poor countries in general, and more FDI in particular, could serve poor countries well. Unfortunately, corruption, administrative inefficiency, and risks of expropriation in many poor countries make a beneficial redirection of international capital flows unlikely before poor countries provide better governance, the rule of law, and economic freedom.

Fourth, it is frequently suggested that rich and democratic countries should provide more economic aid. By and large, big economies, like the US or Japan, provide much less aid than small Scandinavian economies, like Norway or Sweden. But barriers to imports from poor countries are the lowest in the US and the highest in Norway. Whereas European assistance to poor countries is largely provided by governments, American **private** giving might be 3.5 times as high as American official development assistance (Adelman 2003, p. 9). Rich country subsidies to agricultural producers which harm poor countries are much higher than development aid. Whereas EU aid per African person is about 8 dollars, subsidies per EU cow are 913 dollars (UNDP 2003, pp. 155–160). But the theoretical case for aid has always been weak (Bauer 1981). Aid may strengthen governments and undermine free markets. This risk is much greater with government to government aid than with private giving which rarely targets the state as recipient. Certainly, foreign aid does **not** promote democracy (Knack 2004).

Econometric studies have **not** been successful in demonstrating that aid generally increases growth rates. In recent studies one either finds a curvilinear relationship between aid and growth (Hansen and Tarp 2000) which suggests that **some** aid may be useful, but **too much** of it may be harmful, or one finds a conditional effect which suggests that positive aid effects depend on a proper policy environment in the target nation and that elsewhere aid is simply wasted (Burnside and Dollar 2000). The curvilinear relationship builds on the idea that aid may finance useful government spending, but also might have negative incentive effects elsewhere in the economy. If aid is too generous the negative effect might dominate. The conditional effect model argues that the usefulness of aid depends on a context of reasonable fiscal, monetary, and trade policies rather than on the amount of aid provided. These findings not only contradict each other, but – worse still – none of them are robust beyond the previous operationalization of the policy variable or the original and limited samples (Brumm 2003; Easterly, Levine and Roodman 2003; Jensen and Paldam 2004; Ovaska 2003). So, we cannot even be confident that modest amounts of aid given to deserving governments that are committed to reasonable policies work! Another study finds that the effectiveness of aid depends on its bilateral rather than multilateral character (Ram 2003). Both, the disappointing findings about the effectiveness of aid and the poor official aid giving record of the biggest Western economies underline that economic development depends above all on domestic efforts, institutions and policies.

The skepticism about the effects of external assistance to poor countries applies to the International Monetary Fund (IMF) and the World Bank, too. Declining economic freedom frequently has been rewarded by an increase in aid flows (Vasquez 1998). Under such circumstances it is difficult to disagree with Lindsey's (2002, p. 264) sweeping criticism of compulsive lending by the two Washington-based institutions: "Both the IMF and the World Bank routinely extend financial assistance to governments that either have no interest in reform or are unable to pull it off. In so doing, they provide those governments with additional financial breathing space and thus reduce the incentives for making needed changes. Consequently, the end result of their interventions is, all too often, to subvert the spread of pro-market policies." Pro-market ideology might be neutralized by the imperative to keep lending in order to assure institutional survival.

But there is **some** room for beneficial outside influences. The mere existence of prosperous and developed countries generates advantages of backwardness and opportunities for faster growth for less developed countries (Barro and Sala-i-Martin 1995; Bleany and Nishiyama 2002; Olson 1996). They can borrow technology from more highly developed countries and thereby grow faster than the Western pioneers of economic development have done. Japan until the 1970s and thereafter the East Asian tiger economies have used these advantages of backwardness very effectively. Currently, China, India and parts of South East Asia do so.

Catch-up opportunities are enhanced, if poor countries invest in human capital for everyone as China or South Korea or Singapore have done to a much greater degree than India or Indonesia (Drèze and Sen 1995), if they follow an export-oriented development strategy, if they welcome foreign direct investment, **and** if prosperous Western economies provide open markets for poor countries and their products instead of protectionist obstacles.[36] European and Japanese agricultural markets or Western textile and garment markets demonstrate the most persistent unwillingness of rich countries to provide a helping hand to poor countries.

The World Trade Organization's meeting in mid-September 2003 has been a tragedy for poor countries. According to the Economist (2003b, p. 29) and "the World Bank, a successful Doha round could raise the global income by more than $ 500 billion a year by 2015. Over 60 % of that gain would go to poor countries, helping to pull 144 million people out of poverty. While most of the poor countries' gains would come from freer trade among themselves, the reduction of rich country farm subsidies and more open markets in the north would also help." Fortunately, past policy failures of this type may be corrected in future.

---

36 Possibly, even industrial policies or planning do less harm in the phase of catch-up growth than later. See Lindsey (2002, pp. 208ff, 254) on the basic idea behind this conjecture, or Weede (2000) for a set of case studies on planning and its effects in Asia.

Rich countries should avoid to exert pressure on poor countries to commit themselves to misguided policies. Global labor standards are an important example for this. Concerning the minimum wage component of labor standards, the World Bank (1995, p. 75) recognized this years ago: "Those affected by minimum wage provisions in low- and middle-income countries are rarely the most needy. Most of the real poor operate in rural and informal markets in such countries and are not protected by minimum wages. The workers whom minimum wage legislation tries to protect – urban formal workers – already earn much more than the less favored majority. Sometimes the differences are extreme – an urban construction worker in Côte d'Ivoire earns 8.8 times the rural wage rate, and a steel worker in India earns 8.4 times the rural wage…And inasmuch as minimum wage and other regulations discourage formal employment by increasing wage and nonwage costs, they hurt the poor who aspire to formal employment." Concerning India, it has been estimated (Mitra 1998, p. 6) that less than 10 % of the workforce is employed in the formal and privileged sector of the economy. More than 90 % of the workforce stand no chance of benefiting from minimum wages or other labor standards.

Norberg (2001, p. 182) has analyzed the problem of this type of Western demands on developing countries with special clarity: "If we force these countries to raise wages before productivity has been improved, this will mean firms and consumers having to pay more for their manpower than it is currently worth, in which case they will be put out of the running by more productive, better paid workers in the western world... In practice, labour and environmental provisions tell the developing countries: You are too poor to trade with us, and we are not going to trade with you until you have grown rich." One might add: If, therefore, you do not grow to overcome mass poverty, then this is your problem, not ours. Western demands for higher wages in poor countries are nothing but an attempt to raise rival's costs – under the cover of hypocritical humanitarianism.

In essence, I suggest that the best means to export democracy is to export capital and capitalism, thereby promoting economic growth and prosperity, thereby contributing to the establishment of the most important economic background conditions of democracy, i. e., prosperity and some separation of economic and political decision-making. Let capital-owners find out which countries are ready for an economic take-off or an economic miracle. Let them contribute to democratization somewhat later. By contrast, I am not convinced that wars and subsequent regime change should be instruments of choice in the promotion democracy. Admittedly, the procedure worked in Germany as well as in Japan after World War II. But both countries already were industrial power-houses before the war and achieved economic miracles thereafter. Muslim targets are much less promising destinations of successful crusades for democracy. By definition, they are Muslim. There is a strong association between being a Muslim country and being an autocracy. Moreover, most Muslim countries are either poor or oil exporters. Again, both conditions are fairly strongly associated with being an autocracy (Weiffen 2004). Simes (2004, p. 14) has put the likely consequences of democratic crusades well: "Pro-democracy zealotry creates a global backlash that alienates friends, confuses allies and adds new recruits to the ranks of our enemies."

If private Western investors in the pursuit of profit, however, promote growth and prosperity in poor countries and thereby help to overcome one of the most powerful obstacles to democratization, then similar negative side-effects are unlikely. As Wolf (2004, p. 12) has observed, political reforms are more urgently required than new modes of doing business: "The big challenge... is to reconcile a world divided into states of hugely unequal capacities with exploitation of the opportunities for convergence offered by international economic integration. In short, if we want a better world, we need not a different economics, but better politics." If politicians could be persuaded of the merit of doing less – for example, putting up fewer obstacles to trade within or between nations or to desist from trade distorting subsidies – this would frequently result in "better politics".

8. Conclusion

It is argued that war ultimately derives from two causes: from the security dilemma and from territorial issues. Both of them tend to generate irreconcilable conflicts of interest. Such conflicts may be suppressed by the nuclear 'balance of terror' resulting in 'peace through fear' or by overwhelming preponderance resulting in 'peace by strength', or they may be neutralized by changing the character of societies and their ties with each other. Free trade contributes to growth and prosperity which, in turn, promotes democratization. Joint democracy significantly reduces the risk of military disputes and war. In addition, trade and openness directly reduce the risk of military conflict. Globalization facilitates a capitalist peace by promoting prosperity and, ultimately, democracy. The capitalist peace tends to mitigate balance of power effects. It has been supported by American power for decades because America's alliances promoted free trade by decreasing its risks and transaction costs (Gowa 1994; Kindleberger 1973).

Concerning rebellion, political violence and civil war, semi-repressive regimes are most at risk. Avoidance of civil war by autocracy, repression or totalitarianism is not desirable, even if it should work, because totalitarian repression has been even more deadly than war or civil war in the 20th century (Rummel 1994). The democratic domestic peace, however, does not suffer from this disadvantage. Since capitalism and globalization, free trade and foreign investment promote prosperity and thereby democratization, something like a capitalist and democratic civil peace may supplement the capitalist peace between nation-states. Since the pacifying consequences of economic freedom, capitalism and globalization are well supported, the policy conclusions are obvious: Economic freedom should be extended, capitalism should be supported and exported. Thereby one generates the prosperity underwriting those components of the capitalist peace which are frequently called the democratic peace.

What is needed is supporting the economic growth without which poor countries are likely to remain poor and autocratic, violence-prone and war-prone. Although the effectiveness of economic aid is questionable, the West can do a lot for poor countries. We can provide an open door for poor country exports. We can provide a prosperous capitalist model for emulation. We can grow ourselves and thereby provide stronger advantages of backwardness for those others who depend on Western technology and know-how as well as on open Western markets. We must not submit to protectionism and "believing that outsourcing causes unemployment" which according to Drezner (2004, p. 23) "is the economic equivalent to believing that the sun revolves around the earth: intuitively compelling but clearly wrong." Although we need open and vigorous economies in rich countries that provide a model for emulation, technology and open markets to developing countries, the actual performance of many stagnant, semi-socialist and protectionist welfare states in the West – certainly including Germany and much of Continental Europe – leaves much to be desired.

Protectionism implies not only an ultimately self-defeating security policy. It is morally objectionable, because it upholds avoidable poverty and because it is in practice not easily distinguishable from racism. Free trade, however, is based on a cosmopolitan morality, on non-discrimination (see Giersch 1995, p. 24; 2002). Looking for the best deal one can get irrespective of the skin color of the seller is morally preferable to practicing racial solidarity. Moreover, replacing the discriminatory criterion 'skin color' by the color of the passport or citizenship seems no moral improvement to me, but treating business partners as individuals instead of members or non-members of some group is. By and large, the cheaper seller needs the deal more urgently than the more expensive seller. Even from a humanitarian perspective, pure capitalism enjoys some advantages.

The capitalist peace requires capitalism, economic freedom, and prosperity. Promoting the capitalist peace is compatible with a specific interpretation of the linkage between capitalism and inequality which has been well put by Norberg (2001, p. 145): "The world's inequality is due to capitalism.

Not to capitalism having made some groups poor but to making its practitioners wealthy. The uneven distribution of wealth in the world is above all due to the uneven distribution of capitalism." This unevenness, however, generates the advantages of backwardness and the opportunity for catch-up growth.

The long-term relationship between capitalism and economic development has been described by an Indian economist (Bhalla 2002, p. 145) in the following terms: "In 1820, global poverty was close top 84 percent of the world's population, and more than a century later it had declined to 56 percent (in 1929) ... by 1992, only a fifth of the world's population was poor. The number of poor people in the world shows a different trajectory; not until the start of globalization (and consistently high growth rates in China and India) in the 1980s does it begin to decline." Recently, however, economic development in Asia where the majority of mankind lives contributed mightily to the reduction of mass poverty. In Bhalla's (2002, p. 142) view, "Asia saw more than a billion people rise out of poverty in just twenty years – a miracle." Thus, poverty can be reduced. In the long run it even can be overcome.

Promoting capitalism abroad, in still poor countries, requires above all an open door and the practice of capitalism at home. The alternative has been suggested by the former prime minister of Singapore, Lee Kuan Yew, in a speech to the US Congress in the 1980s (The Economist 1993, p. 24):

"The most enduring lesson of history is that ambitious growing countries can expand either by grabbing territory, people and resources, or by trading with other countries. The alternative to free trade is not just poverty, it is war."

References

Adams, Karen Ruth. 2003–2004. 'Attack and Conquer? International Anarchy and the Offense-Defense-Deterrence Balance'. *International Security* 28 (3): 45–83.

Adelman, Carol C. 2003. 'The Privatization of Foreign Aid'. *Foreign Affairs* 82(6): 9–14.

Ahrens, Joachim. 2002. *Governance and Economic Development.* Cheltenham, UK: Edward Elgar.

Aron, Raymond. 1966. 'The Anarchical Order of Power'. *Daedalus* 95: 479–502.

Barbieri, Katherine. 2002. *The Liberal Illusion. Does Trade Promote Peace?* Ann Arbor: The University of Michigan Press. 2003. *'Are Trading States More Peaceful?'* Paper delivered at the 2nd General Conference of the *European Consortium for Political Research,* Marburg (Germany), September 19.

Barbieri, Katherine and Richard Alan Peters. 2003. 'Measure for Mis-measure: A Response to Gartzke and Li'. *Journal of Peace Research* 40(6): 713–719.

Barro, Robert J: and Xavier Sala-i-Martin. 1995. *Economic Growth*. New York: McGraw-Hill.

Bauer, Peter T. 1981. *Equality, the Third World and Economic Delusion*. London: Weidenfeld and Nicolson.

Baumol, William J. 2002. *The Free Market Innovation Machine*. Princeton, NJ: Princeton University Press.

Baumol, William J., Alan S. Blinder, and Edward N. Wolff. 2003. *Downsizing in America. Reality, Causes, and Consequences*. New York: Russell Sage Foundation.

Beck, Nathaniel, Jonathan N. Katz, and Richard Tucker. 1998. 'Taking Time Seriously: Time-Series Cross-Section Analysis with a Binary Dependent Variable'. *American Journal of Political Science* 42(4): 1260–1288.

Beck, Nathaniel, Gary King, and Langche Zeng. 2004. 'Theory and Evidence in International Conflict'. *American Political Science Review* 98(2): 379–389.

Benoit, Kenneth. 1996. 'Democracies Really Are More Pacific (in General)'. *Journal of Conflict Resolution* 40(4): 636–657.

Berggren, Niclas. 2003. 'The Benefits of Economic Freedom'. *The Independent Review* VIII(2): 193–211.

Bernholz, Peter. 1985. *The International Game of Power.* Amsterdam: Mouton.

Betts, Richard K. 1985. 'Conventional Deterrence: Predictive Uncertainty and Policy Confidence'. *World Politics* 37: 159–179.
1987. *Nuclear Blackmail and Nuclear Balance.* Washington, DC: Brookings.

Bhagwati, Jagdish. 1991. *The World Trading System at Risk.* London: Harvester and Wheatsheaf.
1993. 'Democracy and Development'. Pp. 31–38 in Larry Diamond and Marc F. Plattner (eds.): *Capitalism, Socialism and Democracy Revisited.* Baltimore: Johns Hopkins University Press.
2004a. 'Don't Cry for Cancun'. *Foreign Affairs* 83(1): 52–63.
2004b. *In Defense of Globalization.* New York: Oxford University Press.

Bhalla, Surjit S. 2002. *Imagine There's No Country: Poverty, Inequality and Growth in the Era of Globalization.* Washington, DC: Institute for International Economics.

Bleany, Michael and Akira Nishiyama. 2002. 'Explaining Growth'. *Journal of Economic Growth* 7(1): 43–56.

Boix, Carles and Susan C. Stokes. 2003. 'Endogenous Democratization'. *World Politics* 55(4): 517–549.

Boulding, Kenneth E: 1962. *Conflict and Defense.* New York: Harper and Row.

Bremer, Stuart A. 1992. 'Dangerous Dyads: Interstate War, 1816–1965'. *Journal of Conflict Resolution* 36: 309–341.

Stephen G. Brooks and William C. Wolforth. 2002. 'American Primacy in Perspective'. *Foreign Affairs* 81(4): 20–33.

Brumm, Harold J. 2003. 'Aid, Policies, and Growth: Bauer was Right'. *CATO Journal* 23(2): 167–174.

Bueno de Mesquita, Bruce 1981a. *The War Trap.* New Haven, CT: Yale University Press.
1981b. 'Risk, Power Distributions and the Likelihood of War'. *International Studies Quarterly* 25(4): 541–568.

Burkhart, Ross E. and Michael S. Lewis-Beck. 1994. 'Comparative Democracy: The Economic Development Thesis.' *American Political Science Review* 88(4): 903–910.

Burkhart, Ross E. and Indra de Soysa. 2002. 'Open Borders, Open Regimes? FDI, Trade and Democratization, 1970–1999'. Unpublished manuscript. Department of Political Science, *Boise State University, Idaho,* and *Zentrum für Entwicklungsforschung,* Universität Bonn.

Burnside, Craig and David Dollar. 2000. 'Aid, Policies and Growth'. *American Economic Review* 90(4): 847–868.

Campbell, Ian. 2004. 'Retreat from Globalization'. *The National Interest* 75: 111–117.

Chan, Steve. 1984. 'Are Freer Countries More Pacific?' *Journal of Conflict Resolution* 28(4): 617–648.

Cole, Julio H. 2003. 'The Contribution of Economic Freedom to World Economic Growth, 1980–99'. *CATO Journal* 23(2): 189–198.

Collier, Paul and David Dollar. 2002. *Globalization, Growth and Poverty.* New York: Oxford University Press (for the World Bank).

Collier, Paul et al. 2003. *The Conflict Trap.* New York: Oxford University Press.

Collins, Randall. 1986. *Weberian Sociological Theory.* Cambridge: Cambridge University Press.
1995. 'Prediction in Macrosociology: The Case of the Soviet Collapse'. *American Journal of Sociology* 100(6): 1552–1593.

de Haan, Jacob and Clemens L. J. Siermann. 1998. 'Further evidence on the relationship between economic freedom and economic growth'. *Public Choice* 95(3-4): 363-380.

de Haan, Jacob and Jan-Egbert Sturm. 2000. 'On the relationship between economic freedom and economic growth'. *European Journal of Political Economy* 16: 215-241.

de Marchi, Scott, Christopher Gelpi, and Jeffrey D. Grynaviski. 2004. 'Untangling Neural Nets'. *American Political Science Review* 98(2): 371-378.

de Soysa, Indra. 2000. 'The Resource Curse: Are Civil Wars Driven by Rapacity or Paucity? Pp. 113-135 in Mats Berdal and David M. Malone (eds.): *Greed and Grievance. Economic Agendas in Civil War.* Boulder, CO: Lynne Rienner.
2002. Paradise is a Bazaar. Greed, Creed and Grievance in Civil War, 1989-1999.' *Journal of Peace Research* 39(4): 395-410.
2003. *Foreign Direct Investment, Democracy and Development.* London: Routledge.

de Soysa, Indra and John R. Oneal. 1999. 'Boon or Bane? Reassessing the Productivity of Foreign Direct Investment'. *American Sociological Review* 64(5): 766-782.

de Soysa, Indra and Angelika Wagner. 2003. 'Global Market, Local Mayhem? Foreign Investment, Trade Openness, State Capacity and Civil War, 1989-2000.' Paper presented at the *International Studies Association Convention*, Portland, Oregon, February.

Deutsch, Karl W. and J. David Singer. 1964. 'Multipolar Power Systems and International Security'. *World Politics* 16: 390–406.

Dixon, William J. 1993. 'Democracy and the Management of International Conflict'. *Journal of Conflict Resolution* 37(1): 42–68.

Dollar, David. 1992. 'Outward-Oriented Developing Economies Really Do Grow More Rapidly'. *Economic Development and Cultural Change* 40(3): 523–544.

Dollar, David and Aart Kraay. 2002. 'Spreading the Wealth'. *Foreign Affairs* 81(1): 120–133.

Doucouliagos, Chris and Mehmet Ulubasoglu. 2003. 'Economic Freedom and Economic Growth'. Paper presented at the *European Public Choice Society Meeting*, Berlin, April 18.

Doyle, Michael W. 1993. 'Politics and Grand Strategy.' Pp. 22–47 in Richard Rosecrance and Arthur A. Stein (eds.): *The Domestic Bases of Grand Strategy*. Ithaca, NY: Cornell University Press.

Dreze, Jean and Armatya Sen. 1995. *India: Economic Development and Social Opportunity*. Delhi: Oxford University Press.

Drezner, Daniel W. 2004. 'The Outsourcing Bogeyman'. *Foreign Affairs* 83(3): 22–34.

Dupuy, Trevor N. 1987. *Understanding War.* New York: Paragon.

Easterly, William, Ross Levine and David Roodman. 2003. 'New Data, New Doubts: A Comment on Burnside and Dollar's "Aid, Policies, and Growth" (2000)'. Cambridge, MA: *National Bureau of Economic Research,* Working Paper 9846.

Economist, The. 1993. 'Survey: Asia. A billion consumers'. *The Economist* 329, No. 7835, October 30th.
2003a. 'Flying on one engine. A Survey of the World Economy'. *The Economist* 368, No. 8342, September 20th.
2003b. 'Trade Policy: Bras, bolts and Brazil'. The Economist 369, No. 8351, November 22nd: 51–52.
2004a. 'More or less equal?' *The Economist* 370, No. 8366, March 13th: 73–75.
2004b. 'Oh, sweet reason'. *The Economist* 371, No. 8371, April 17th: 73.
2004c. 'In need of a makeover. A Survey of California'. *The Economist* 371, No. 8373, May 1st.
2004d. 'China's growing pains'. *The Economist* 372, No. 8389, August 21st: 11–12.

Economy, Elizabeth. 2004. 'Don't Break the Engagement'. *Foreign Affairs* 83(3): 96–109.

Edwards, Sebastian. 1998. Openness, Productivity and Growth. What Do We Really Know? *Economic Journal* 108: 383–398.

Epstein, Joshua M. 1988. 'Dynamic Analysis of the Conventional Balance in Europe'. *International Security* 12(4): 154–168.

Farr, W. Ken, Richard A. Lord, and J. Larry Wolfenbarger. 1998. 'Economic Freedom, Political Freedom, and Economic Well-Being: A Causal Analysis'. *CATO Journal* 18(2): 247–262.

Fearon, James D. and David D. Laitin. 2003. 'Ethnicity, Insurgency, and Civil War'. *American Political Science Review* 97(1): 75–90.
2004. 'Neotrusteeship and the Problem of Weak States'. *International Security* 28(4): 5–43.

Finsterbusch, Stephan. 2003. 'Taiwan zeigt China den Weg in den Kapitalismus'. *Frankfurter Allgemeine Zeitung* 273, Montag, November 24: 14.

Fu, Zhengyuan. 1993. *Autocratic Tradition and Chinese Politics.* Cambridge: Cambridge University Press.

Gallagher, Mary E. 2002. 'Reform and Openness: Why China's Economic Reforms Have Delayed Democracy'. *World Politics* 54(3): 338–372.

Gartzke, Erik. 2000. 'Preferences and the Democratic Peace'. *International Studies Quarterly* 44(2): 191–212.
2004. 'The Futility of War. Capitalism and Common Interests as Determinants of the Democratic Peace'. Manuscript, Department of Political Science, Columbia University.

Gartzke, Erik and Quan Li. 2003a. 'Measure for Measure: Concept Operationalization and the Trade Interdependence – Conflict Debate'. *Journal of Peace Research* 40(5): 553–571.
2003b. 'War, Peace and the Invisible Hand'. *International Studies Quarterly* 47(4): 561–586.
2003c. 'All's Well That Ends Well. A Reply to Oneal, Barbieri and Peters'. *Journal of Peace Research* 40(6): 727–732.

Geller, Dan S. 1992. 'Capability Concentration, Power Transition and War'. *International Interactions* 17: 269–284.

Geller, Dan S. and J. David Singer. 1998. *Nations at War.* Cambridge: Cambridge University Press.

Giersch, Herbert. 1995/2002. *Wirtschaftsmoral als Standortfaktor.* Jena: Max Planck Institute for Economic Research. Also: 'Economic Morality as a Competitive Asset'. Pp. 444–469 in Geoffrey Brennan, Hartmut Kliemt and Robert Tollison (eds.): *Method and Morals in Constitutional Economics. Essays in Honor of James M. Buchanan.* Berlin: Springer.

Gilboy, George J. 2004. 'The Myth Behind China's Miracle'. *Foreign Affairs* 83(4): 33-48.

Gilpin, Robert W. 1981. *War and Change in World Politics.* Cambridge: Cambridge University Press.

Gleditsch, Nils Petter, Peter Wallensteen, Mikael Eriksson, Margareta Sollenberg, and Harvard Strand. 2002. 'Armed Conflict 1946-2001: A New Dataset'. *Journal of Peace Research* 39(5): 615-637.

Goertz; Gary and Paul F. Diehl. 1992. *Territorial Changes and International Conflict.* London: Routledge.

Goldstein, Lyle J. 2003. 'When China was a Rogue State: the impact of China's nuclear weapons program on US-China relations during the 1960s'. *Journal of Contemporary China* 12(37): 739-764.

Gowa, Joanne. 1994. *Allies, Adversaries, and International Trade.* Princeton: Princeton University Press.
1999. *Ballots and Bullets. The Elusive Democratic Peace.* Princeton: Princeton University Press.

Gurr, T. R. 1968. 'A Causal Model of Civil Strife'. *American Political Science Review* 62(4): 1104-1124.
1970. *Why Men Rebel.* Princeton: Princeton University Press.

(ed.) 1980. *Handbook of Political Conflict*. New York: Free Press.

Gwartney, James and Robert Lawson. 2003. *Economic Freedom of the World. 2003 Annual Report.* Vancouver, BC: Fraser Institute, and Potsdam: Friedrich Naumann Foundation. 2004. *Economic Freedom of the World. 2004 Annual Report.* Vancouver, BC: Fraser Institute, and Potsdam: Friedrich Naumann Foundation.

Gwartney, James, Robert Lawson, and Dexter Samida. 2000. *Economic Freedom of the World. 2000 Annual Report.* Vancouver, BC: Fraser Institute, and Potsdam: Friedrich Naumann Foundation.

Hale, David. 2004. 'China's Growing Appetites'. *The National Interest* 76: 137–147.

Hansen, Henrik and Finn Tarp. 2000. 'Aid Effectiveness Disputed'. Pp. 103–128 in Finn Tarp (ed.): *Foreign Aid and Development*. London: Routledge.

Harff, Barbara. 2003. 'No Lessons Learned from the Holocaust? Assessing the Risks of Genocide and Political Mass Murder since 1955'. *American Political Science Review* 97(1): 57–73.

Harrelson-Stephens, Julie and Rhonda L. Callaway. 2003. 'Does Trade Openness Promote Security Rights in

Developing Countries?' *International Interactions* 29(2): 143–158.

Hayek, Friedrich August von. 1945. 'The Use of Knowledge in Society'. *American Economic Review* 35(4): 519–530.
1960/1971. *The Constitution of Liberty.* Chicago: University of Chicago Press. Also: *Die Verfassung der Freiheit.* Tübingen: Mohr Siebeck.

Hegre, Harvard. 2000. 'Development and the Liberal Peace: What Does it Take to be a Trading State?' *Journal of Peace Research* 37(1): 5–30.
2003. 'Disentangling Democracy and Development as Determinants of Armed Conflict', Paper presented at the Annual Meeting of the *International Studies Association,* Portland, OR, February 25 – March 1.
2004. 'Size Asymmetry, Trade, and Militarized Conflict'. *Journal of Conflict Resolution* 48(3): 403–429.

Hegre, Harvard, Tanja Ellingsen, Scott Gates, and Nils Petter Gleditsch. 2001. 'Toward a Democratic Civil Peace? Democracy, Political Change, and Civil War, 1816–1992'. *American Political Science Review* 95(1): 33–48.

Hegre, Harvard, Ranveig Gissinger, and Nils Petter Gleditsch. 2003. 'Globalization and Internal Conflict'. Pp. 251–275 in Gerald Schneider, Katherine Barbieri and Nils Petter Gleditsch (eds.): *Globalization and Armed Conflict.* Lanham, MD: Rowman and Littlefield.

Henderson, Errol A. and Singer, David J. 2000. 'Civil War in the Post-Colonial World, 1946-92'. *Journal of Peace Research* 37(3): 275-299.

Herz, John H. 1950. 'Idealist Internationalism and the Security Dilemma'. *World Politics* 2(2): 157-180.

Hewitt, J. Joseph. 2003. 'Dyadic Processes and International Crises'. *Journal of Conflict Resolution* 47(5): 669-692.

Hobson, John M. 1997. *The Wealth of States. A Comparative Sociology of International Economic and Political Change.* Cambridge: Cambridge University Press.

Huntington, Samuel P. 2004. 'Dead Souls. The Denationalization of the American Elite'. *The National Interest* 75: 5-18.

Irwin, Douglas A. 2002. *Free Trade Under Fire.* Princeton: Princeton University Press.

Jensen, Peter Sandholt and Martin Paldam. 2004. 'Can the new aid-growth models be replicated?' Paper presented at the *European Public Choice Society Meeting,* Berlin, April 16.

Jones, Eric L. 1981/1991. *The European Miracle.* Cambridge: Cambridge University Press/*Das Wunder Europa.* Tübingen: Mohr Siebeck.
1988. *Growth Recurring.* Oxford: Oxford University Press.

Kahneman, Daniel and Amos Tversky. 1979. 'Prospect Theory: An Analysis of Decisions under Risk'. *Econometrica* 47: 263–291.

Kant, Immanuel. 1795/1963/1964. *Zum ewigen Frieden.* Translation in Lewis White Beck (ed.), *Kant on History.* New York: Macmillan 1963. Wieder abgedruckt in I. Kant: Schriften zur Anthropologie, Geschichtsphilosophie, Politik und Pädagogik (Bd. 6 der Werke). Darmstadt: Wissenschaftliche Buchgesellschaft 1964.

Kaplan, Morton A. 1957. *System and Process in International Politics.* New York: Wiley.

Kasper, Wolfgang. 2004. 'Freedom and Economic Development: Applying the Lessons'. Paper presented at the *Mont Pelerin Society Regional Meeting, Sri Lanka,* January 10–15.

Kim, Woosang. 1992. 'Power Transitions and Great Power War from Westphalia to Waterloo'. *World Politics* 45: 153–172.

Kindleberger, Charles. 1973. *The World in Depression, 1929–1939.* Berkeley: University of California Press.

Knack, Stephen. 2004. 'Does Foreign Aid Promote Democracy?' *International Studies Quarterly* 48(1): 251–266.

Kristof, Nicholas D. and Sheryl WuDunn. 1994. *China Wakes.* New York: Random House.

Krugman, Paul. 1996. *Pop Internationalism.* Cambridge, MA: MIT Press.

Kugler, Jacek and Douglas Lemke (eds.). 1996. *Parity and War.* Ann Arbor: The University of Michigan Press.

Kugler, Jacek and A.F.K. Organski. 1993.'The Power Transition'. Pp. 142–194 in Manus I. Midlarsky (ed.): *Handbook of War Studies,* 2nd ed. Ann Arbor, MI: University of Michigan Press.

Kuhn, Thomas S. 1962. *The Structure of Scientific Revolutions.* Chicago: The University of Chicago Press.

Lakatos, Imre. 1968–1969. 'Criticism and the Methodology of Scientific Research Programmes'. *Proceedings of the Aristotelian Society* 69: 149–186.

Lal, Deepak. 2003. 'In Defence of Empires'. *Economic Affairs* 23(4): 14–19.

Lampton, David M. 2003. 'The Stealth Normalization of U.S.-China Relations'. *The National Interest* 73: 37–48.

Landes, David S. 1998. *The Wealth and Poverty of Nations.* New York: Norton.

Lemke, Douglas. 2002. *Regions of War and Peace.* Cambridge: Cambridge University Press.
2003. 'Investigating the Preventive Motive for War'. *International Interactions* 29(4): 273–292.

Lindert, Peter H. 2004. *Growing Public. Social Spending and Economic Growth Since the Eighteenth Century.* Cambridge: Cambridge University Press.

Lindert, Peter H. and Jeffrey G. Williamson. 2001. 'Does Globalization Make the World More Unequal?' *NBER Working Paper* 8228 (Cambridge, MA).

Lindsey, Brink. 2002. *Against the Dead Hand. The Uncertain Struggle for Global Capitalism.* New York: Wiley.

Lipset, Seymour Martin. 1994. 'The Social Requisites of Democracy Revisited'. *American Sociological Review* 59(1): 1–22.

Lipson, Charles. 2003. *Reliable Partners. How Democracies Have Made a Separate Peace.* Princeton: Princeton University Press.

Maoz, Zeev and Bruce M. Russett. 1993. 'Normative and Structural Causes of the Democratic Peace'. *American Political Science Review* 87(3): 624–638.

Maddison, Angus. 1998. *Chinese Economic Performance in the Long-Run.* Paris: OECD.

Mansfield, Edward D. and Jon C. Pevehouse. 2003. 'Institutions, Interdependence, and International Conflict'. Pp. 233–250 in Gerald Schneider, Katherine Barbieri, and Nils Petter Gleditsch (eds.): *Globalization and Armed Conflict.* Lanham, MD: Rowman and Littlefield.

Mearsheimer, John J. 2001. *The Tragedy of Great Power Politics.* New York: Norton.

Mehlkop, Guido. 2002. *Wirtschaftliche Freiheit, Einkommensungleichheit und physische Lebensqualität.* Opladen: Leske und Budrich.

Michels, Robert. 1910/1970. *Zur Soziologie des Parteiwesens.* Stuttgart: Kröner.

Mitra, Barun S. 1998. 'Democracy, Equity and the Market'. Pp. 5–13 in Tibor R. Machan and Barun S. Mitra: *Democracy, Market and Human Rights.* New Delhi: Liberty Institute.

Modelski, George and William R. Thompson. 1993. 'Long Cycles and Global War'. Pp. 23–54 in Manus I. Midlarsky (ed.): *Handbook of War Studies,* 2nd ed. Ann Arbor, MI: University of Michigan Press.

Moul, William Brian. 1992. 'Polarity, Balance of Power and War'. *International Interactions* 18(2): 165–193.
2003. 'Power Parity, Preponderance and War between Great Powers'. *Journal of Conflict Resolution* 47(4): 468–489.

Mousseau, Michael, Harvard Hegre, and John R. Oneal. 2003. 'How the Wealth of Nations Conditions the Liberal Peace'. *European Journal of International Relations* 9(2): 277–314.

Mueller, Dennis C. and Thomas Stratmann. 2003. 'The economic effects of democratic participation.' *Journal of Public Economics* 87: 2129–2155.

Muller, Edward N. 1985. Income Inequality, Regime Repressiveness and Political Violence. *American Political Science Review* 50(1): 47–61.

Muller, Edward N. and Erich Weede. 1990. 'Cross-National Variation in Political Violence. A Rational Choice Approach'. *Journal of Conflict Resolution* 34(4): 624–651. 1993. 'Ungleichheit, Deprivation und Gewalt'. *Kölner Zeitschrift für Soziologie und Sozialpsychologie* 45(1): 41–45.

Noland, Marcus, Li Gang-Liu, Sherman Robinson and Zhi Wang. 1998. *Global Economic Effects of the Asian Currency Devaluations.* Washington, DC: Institute for international Economics.

Norberg, Johan. 2001. *In Defence of Global Capitalism.* Stockholm: Timbro.

North, Douglas C. 1981. *Structure and Change in Economic History.* New York: Norton.

1990. *Institutions, Institutional Change and Economic Performance.* Cambridge: Cambridge University Press.

Oberschall, Anthony. 1997. *Social Movements: Ideologies, Interests and Identities.* New Brunswick, NJ: Transaction.

O'Driscoll, Gerald P., Kim R. Holmes, and Melanie Kirkpatrick. 2001. *Index of Economic Freedom.* New York: Wall Street Journal, and Washington, DC: Heritage Foundation.

OECD. 1998. *Open Markets Matter. The Benefits of Trade and Investment Liberalisation.* Paris: Organisation for Economic Co-operation and Development.

Olson, Mancur. 1965/1968. *The Logic of Collective Action.* Cambridge, MA: Harvard University Press/*Die Logik des kollektiven Handelns.* Tübingen: Mohr Siebeck.
1996. 'Big Bills Left on the Sidewalk: Why Some Nations are Rich, and Others Poor'. *Journal of Economic Perspectives* 10(2): 3–24.

Oneal, John R. 2003. 'Measuring Interdependence and Its Pacific Benefits'. *Journal of Peace Research* 40(6): 721–725.

Oneal, John R. and Bruce Russett. 1997. 'The Classical Liberals Were Right: Democracy, Interdependence, and Conflict, 1950–1985'. *International Studies Quarterly* 40(2): 267–294.

1999. 'The Kantian Peace: The Pacific Benefits of Democracy, Interdependence, and International Organizations, 1885–1992'. *World Politics* 52(1): 1–37.

2003a. 'Assessing the Liberal Peace with Alternative Specifications'. Pp. 143–163 in Gerald Schneider, Katherine Barbieri and Nils Petter Gleditsch (eds.): *Globalization and Armed Conflict*. Lanham, MD: Rowman and Littlefield.

2003b. 'Modelling Conflict While Studying Dynamics'. Pp. 179–188 in Gerald Schneider, Katherine Barbieri and Nils Petter Gleditsch (eds.): *Globalization and Armed Conflict*. Lanham, MD: Rowman and Littlefield.

Oneal, John R., Bruce Russett, and Michael L. Berbaum. 2003. 'Causes of Peace: Democracy, Interdependence, and International Organizations, 1885–1992'. *International Studies Quarterly* 47(3): 371–393.

Organski, A.F.K. 1958. *World Politics*. New York: A. A. Knopf.

Organski, A.F.K. and Jacek Kugler. 1980. *The War Ledger*. Chicago: Chicago University Press.

Ovaska, Tomi. 2003. 'The Failure of Development Aid'. *CATO Journal* 23(2): 175–188.

Owen, John M. 1994. 'How Liberalism Produces Democratic Peace'. *International Security* 19(2): 87–125.

Payne, James L. 1989. *Why Nations Arm*. Oxford: Basil Blackwell.

Peceny, Mark, Caroline C. Beer, with Shannon Sanchez-Terry. 2002. 'Dictatorial Peace?' *American Political Science Review* 96(1): 15–26.

Pei, Minxin. 1998. 'Is China Democratizing?' *Foreign Affairs* 77(1): 68–82.

Pipes, Richard. 1999. *Property and Freedom*. New York: A. A. Knopf.

Popper, Karl R. 1934/1959. *Die Logik der Forschung*. Tübingen: Mohr Siebeck/*The Logic of Scientific Discovery*. London: Hutchinson.

Przeworski, Adam, Michael E. Alvarez, Jose Antonio Cheibub and Fernando Limongi. 2000. *Democracy and Development*. Cambridge: Cambridge University Press.

Quinlan, Joseph P. 2002. 'Ties That Bind'. *Foreign Affairs* 81(4): 116–126.

Ram, Rati. 2003. 'Roles of Bilateral and Multilateral Aid in Economic Growth of Developing Countries'. *Kyklos* 56(1): 95–110.

Ravallion, Martin. 2004. 'Pessimistic on poverty?' *The Economist* 371, No. 8370, April 10th: 70.

Ray, James L. 1995. *Democracy and International Conflict.* Columbia, SC: University of South Carolina Press.
2003. 'Explaining Interstate Conflict and War'. *Conflict Management and Peace Science* 20(2): 1–31.

Rodrik Dani. 1998. 'Why Do More Open Economies Have Bigger Governments?' *Journal of Political Economy* 106(5): 997–1032.

Rogowski, Ronald. 1990. *Commerce and Coalitions: How Trade Affects Domestic Political Alignments.* Princeton: Princeton University Press.

Ross, Michael L. 2004. 'How Do Natural Resources Influence Civil War?' *International Organization* 58(1): 35–67.

Rowen, Henry S. 1996. 'China: A Short March to Democracy'. *The National Interest* 45: 61–70.

Rule, James B. 1988. *Theories of Civil Violence.* Berkeley: University of California Press.

Rummel, Rudolph J. 1994. *Death by Government.* New Brunswick, N J: Transaction.
1995. 'Democracies ARE Less Warlike Than Other

Regimes'. *European Journal of International Relations* 1(4): 457–479.

Russett, Bruce M. 1993. *Grasping the Democratic Peace.* Princeton: Princeton University Press.

Russett, Bruce M. and John R. Oneal. 2001. *Triangulating Peace. Democracy, Interdependence and International Organizations.* New York: W. W. Norton.

Sachs, Jeffrey D. and Andrew M. Warner. 1997. 'Sources of Slow Growth in African Economies'. *Journal of African Economies* 6: 335–376.

Sandschneider, Eberhard. 1998. 'Die Kommunistische Partei Chinas an der Macht'. Pp. 169–185 in Carsten Hermann-Pillath und Michael Lackner (eds.): *Länderbericht China.* Bonn: Bundeszentrale für Politische Bildung.

Schumpeter, Joseph A. 1942. *Capitalism, Socialism and Democracy.* New York: Harper and Brothers.

Simes, Dimitri. 2004. 'Iraq at the Turn: Rethinking the Strategy'. *The National Interest* 76: 11–14.

Singer, J. David, Stuart Bremer and John Stuckey. 1972. 'Capability Distribution, Uncertainty and Major Power War, 1820–1965'. Pp. 19–48 in Bruce M. Russett (ed.): *Peace, War and Numbers.* Beverly Hills, CA: Sage.

Skocpol, Theda. 1976. 'France, Russia, China: A Structural Analysis of Social Revolutions'. *Comparative Studies in Society and History* 18: 175–210.

Smith, Adam. 1776/1976/1990. *An Inquiry into the Nature and Causes of the Wealth of Nations.* Oxford: Oxford University Press/*Der Wohlstand der Nationen.* München: DTV.

Snyder, Jack. 1991. *Myths of Empire: Domestic Politics and International Ambition.* Ithaca, NY: Cornell University Press.

Stein, Arthur A. 1990. *Why Nations Cooperate.* Ithaca, NY: Cornell University Press.

Sweeney, Kevin J. 2003. 'Are Dyadic Preponderances Really More Pacific?' *Journal of Conflict Resolution* 47(6): 728–750.

Theurl, Theresa. 1999. 'Globalisierung als Selektionsprozeß ordnungspolitischer Paradigmen'. Pp. 23–45 in Hartmut Berg (ed.): *Globalisierung der Wirtschaft : Ursachen – Formen – Konsequenzen.* Berlin: Duncker und Humblot.

Tullock, Gordon. 1974. *The Social Dilemma. The Economics of War and Revolution.* Blacksburg, VA: University Publications.

Tures, John A. 2003. 'Economic Freedom and Conflict Reduction: Evidence from the 1970, 1980s, and 1990s'. *CATO Journal* 22(3): 533–542.

UNDP. 2003. *Human Development Report 2003*. New York: Oxford University Press (for the United Nations Development Programme).

Vasquez, Ian. 1998. 'Official Assistance, Economic Freedom, and Policy Change'. *CATO Journal* 18(2): 275–286.

Vasquez, John A. 1993. *The War Puzzle*. Cambridge: Cambridge University Press.

Vega-Gordillo, Manuel and José L. Alvarez-Arce. 2003. 'Economic Growth and Freedom: A Causal Study'. *CATO Journal* 23(2): 199–215.

Wade, Robert. 1996. 'Globalization and its Limits: Reports of the Death of the National Economy are Greatly Exaggerated'. Pp. 60–88 in Suzanne Berger and Ronald Dore (eds.): *National Diversity and Global Capitalism*. Ithaca, NY: Cornell University Press.

Waltz, Kenneth N. 1979. *Theory of International Politics*. Reading, MA: Addison-Wesley.
2003–2004. 'Fair Fights or Pointless Wars'. *International Security* 28(3): 181.

Wang, Kevin and James Lee Ray. 1994. 'Beginners and Winners: The Fate of Initiators of Interstate Wars Involving Great Powers Since 1495'. *International Studies Quarterly* 38: 139–154.

Weede, Erich. 1975. *Weltpolitik und Kriegsursachen im 20. Jahrhundert.* München: Oldenbourg.
1983. 'Extended Deterrence by Superpower Alliance'. *Journal of Conflict Resolution* 27: 231–253 and 739 (where misprints are corrected).
1984. 'Democracy and War Involvement'. *Journal of Conflict Resolution* 28(4): 649–664.
1986. 'Income Inequality and Violence Reconsidered'. *American Sociological Review* 51: 438–441.
1996. *Economic Development, Social Order, and World Politics.* Boulder, CO: Lynne Rienner.
1998. 'Are Rebellion and Transfer of Power Determined by Relative Deprivation or by Rational Choice?' *Guru Nanak Journal of Sociology* 19(2): 1–33.
2000. Asien und der Westen. Baden-Baden: Nomos.
2001/2002. 'Südkorea und Rußland: Wie man Wohlstand erarbeitet oder verspielt'. *Ordo* 52: 175–187. Also: 'Korea and Russia: How to Grow Rich or to Remain Poor'. Pacific Focus XVII(1): 67–82.
2002. 'The Transition to Capitalism in China and Russia'. *Comparative Sociology* 1(2): 151–167.
2004a. 'On Political Violence and Its Avoidance'. *Acta Politica:* 39(2): 152–178.
2004b. 'The Diffusion of Prosperity and Peace by Globalization'. *The Independent Review* 9(2): 165–186.

Weede, Erich and Sebastian Kämpf. 2002. 'The Impact of Intelligence and Institutional Improvements on Economic Growth'. *Kyklos* 55(3): 361–380.

Weede, Erich and Edward N. Muller. 1997. 'Consequences of Revolutions'. *Rationality and Society* 9(3): 327–350.
1998. 'Rebellion, Violence and Revolution: A Rational Choice Perspective'. *Journal of Peace Research* 35(1): 43–59.

Weiffen, Brigitte. 2004. 'The interplay of culture and economy: Impediments to democracy in the Middle East'. Paper presented at the *36th World Congress of the International Institute of Sociology,* Beijing, July 7–11.

Weingast, Barry R. 1995. 'The Economic Role of Political Institutions: Market-Preserving Federalism and Economic Development'. *Journal of Law, Economics, and Organization* 11(1): 1–31.

Wolf, Martin. 2004. *Why Globalization Works.* New Haven, CT: Yale University Press.

Wood, Adrian. 1994. *North-South Trade, Employment and Inequality.* Oxford: Oxford University Press (Clarendon).

World Bank. 1995. *World Development Report 1995.* New York: Oxford University Press.
2003. *World Development Report 2004.* New York: Oxford University Press.

Zakaria, Fareed. 2003. *The Future of Freedom.* New York: Norton.

Zinnes, Dina A. 2004. 'Constructing Political Logic: The Democratic Peace Puzzle'. *Journal of Conflict Resolution* 48(3): 430–454.

Biographical Note

Until fall 2004, Erich Weede has been professor of sociology at the University of Bonn, Germany. His research interests have included quantitative studies of war and violence since the 1970s, cross-national studies of economic growth and income inequality since the 1980s, and historical patterns of Asian and Western development in the last millennium since the 1990s. He is author of about 180 contributions to American, Asian, and European publications as well as ten books, including *Weltpolitik und Kriegsursachen im 20. Jahrhundert* (Oldenbourg, München 1975), *Economic Development, Social Order and World Politics* (Lynne Rienner, Boulder, CO 1996), *Asien und der Westen: Politische und kulturelle Determinanten der wirtschaftlichen Entwicklung* (Nomos, Baden-Baden 2000), *Mensch, Markt und Staat: Plädoyer für eine Wirtschaftsordnung für unvollkommene Menschen* (für die Ludwig-Erhard-Stiftung, Lucius et Lucius, Stuttgart 2003). He is a member of the editorial boards of *International Interactions, Journal of Conflict Resolution, New Asia,* and *Pacific Focus.* In 1983, he was President of the *Peace Science Society (International),* and in 1986 Vice-President of the *International Studies Association.* In Winter 1986–87, he was Visiting Professor of International Relations at the Bologna

Center of The Johns Hopkins University. In September 2004, he received the *'Lewis Fry Richardson Lifetime Achievement Award'* from the Standing Group on International Relations of the European Consortium for Political Research.